PRAXIS Special Education:
Core Knowledge and Applications
0354/5354
Practice Test Kit

By: Sharon Wynne, M.S.

XAMonline, Inc.
Boston

Copyright © 2014 XAMonline, Inc.
All rights reserved. No part of the material protected by this copyright notice may be reproduced or utilized in any form or by any means, electronic or mechanical, including photocopying, recording or by any information storage and retrievable system, without written permission from the copyright holder.

To obtain permission(s) to use the material from this work for any purpose including workshops or seminars, please submit a written request to:

XAMonline, Inc.
21 Orient Avenue
Melrose, MA 02176
Email: info@xamonline.com
Web: www.xamonline.com
Phone:1-800-301-4647
Fax: 617-583-5552

Library of Congress Cataloging-in-Publication Data

Wynne, Sharon A.
Praxis Special Education 0354/5354 Practice Test Kit: Teacher Certification /
Sharon A. Wynne 1st edition   ISBN: 978-1-60787-401-0
1. Praxis Special Education Test   2. Study Guides.   3. PRAXIS
4. Teachers' Certification & Licensure   5. Careers

Disclaimer:
The opinions expressed in this publication are the sole works of XAMonline and were created independently from the State Department of Education or other testing affiliates.

Sample test questions are developed by XAMonline and are not former tests. XAMonline makes no claims nor guarantees teacher candidates a passing score.

Printed in the United States of America
Praxis Special Education 0354/5354 Practice Test Kit
ISBN: 978-1-60787-401-0

PRAXIS Special Education Practice Test Kit
Table of Contents

Pre-Test .... Page 4

Pre-Test with Rationales .... Page 34

Pre-Test Answer Key .... Page 103

Pre-Test Rigor Table .... Page 105

Post-Test .... Page 106

Post-Test with Rationales .... Page 135

Post-Test Answer Key .... Page 200

Post-Test Rigor Table .... Page 202

PRAXIS Special Education Practice Test Kit
Pre-Test Sample Questions

1. All of the following EXCEPT one are characteristics of a student who is Emotionally Disturbed:
   (Average)

   A. Socially accepted by peers

   B. Highly disruptive to the classroom environment

   C. Academic difficulties

   D. Areas of talent overlooked by a teacher

2. Which of these characteristics is NOT included in the IDEA definition of emotional disturbance?
   (Rigorous)

   A. General pervasive mood of unhappiness or depression

   B. Social maladjustment manifested in a number of settings

   C. Tendency to develop physical symptoms, pains, or fear associated with school or personal problems

   D. Inability to learn that is not attributed to intellectual, sensory, or health factors

3. Truancy, gang membership, and a feeling of pride in belonging to a delinquent subculture are indicative of:
   (Average)

   A. Conduct disorder

   B. Personality disorders

   C. Immaturity

   D. Socialized aggression

4. Indirect requests and attempts to influence or control others through one's use of language is an example of:
   (Rigorous)

   A. Morphology

   B. Syntax

   C. Pragmatics

   D. Semantics

5. Scott is in middle school but still makes statements like, "I gotted new high-tops yesterday," and "I saw three mans in the front office." Language interventions for Scott would target:
   (Average)

   A. Morphology

   B. Syntax

   C. Pragmatics

   D. Semantics

6. Which component of language involves language content rather than the form of language?
   (Rigorous)

   A. Phonology

   B. Morphology

   C. Semantics

   D. Syntax

7. Which of the following characteristics is probably most related to physical impairments?
   (Rigorous)

   A. Lack of physical stamina

   B. Progressive weakening of muscles

   C. Impaired motor abilities

   D. Side effects from treatment

8. Jennifer is eight years old and has been diagnosed with intellectual disabilities. She exhibits the following characteristics: poor motor development, minimal speech and communication, is not potty trained, and requires constant supervision. How would she be classified in terms of degree of cognitive impairment?
   (Rigorous)

   A. Mild

   B. Moderate

   C. Severe

   D. Profound

9. Otumba is a 16 year old in your class who recently came from Nigeria. The girls in your class have come to you to complain about the way he treats them in a sexist manner. When they complain you reflect that this is also the way he treats adult females. You have talked to Otumba before about appropriate behavior. You should first:
   (Rigorous)

   A. Complain to the Principal

   B. Ask for a Parent-Teacher Conference

   C. Check to see if this is a cultural norm in his country

   D. Create a behavior contract for him to follow

10. Some of the factors that can contribute to learning disabilities and/or cognitive impairments include problems with fetal brain development, genetic factors, environmental factors, problems during pregnancy or delivery, environmental toxins, and the use of drugs or alcohol during pregnancy. Which of the following conditions can be directly related to one of the above listed factors?
    (Easy)

    A. Emotional Disturbance

    B. Fetal Alcohol Syndrome

    C. Learning Disability

    D. Attention Deficit Disorder

11. Statements like, "Darren is lazy," are not helpful in describing his behavior for all but which of these reasons?
    (Rigorous)

    A. There is no way to determine if any change occurs from the information given

    B. The student and not the behavior becomes labeled

    C. Darren's behavior will manifest itself clearly enough without any written description

    D. Such labels are open to various interpretations among the people who are asked to define them

12. Criteria for choosing behaviors that most need change involve all but the following:
    (Average)

    A. Observations across settings to rule out certain interventions

    B. Pinpointing the behavior that is the poorest fit in the child's environment

    C. The teacher's concern about what is the most important behavior to target

    D. Analysis of the environmental reinforcers

13. Measuring frequency is appropriate for all of these behaviors EXCEPT:
    (Rigorous)

    A. Teasing

    B. Talking out

    C. Being on time for class

    D. Off-task behavior

14. **Which is generally true about students with mild disabilities?**
    (Easy)

    A. Comprise about half of the total special education population

    B. Are generally recognized once they begin school and have learning challenges

    C. Have a high school dropout rate

    D. All of the above

15. **Which of the following is true about autism?**
    (Rigorous)

    A. It is caused by having cold, aloof or hostile parents

    B. Approximately 4 out of 10 people have autism

    C. It is a Separate Exceptionality Category in IDEA

    D. It is a form of Mental Illness

16. **In which of the following exceptionality categories may a student be considered for inclusion if his IQ score falls more than two standard deviations below the mean?**
    (Average)

    A. Intellectual Disabilities

    B. Specific Learning Disabilities

    C. Emotionally/Behaviorally Disordered

    D. Gifted

17. **According to IDEA, a child whose disability is related to being deaf and blind may not be classified as:**
    (Rigorous)

    A. Multiple Disabilities

    B. Other Health Impaired

    C. Mentally Retarded

    D. Visually Impaired

18. Legislation in Public Law 94 – 142 attempts to:
    (Average)

    A. Match the child's educational needs with appropriate educational services

    B. Include parents in the decisions made about their child's education

    C. Establish a means by which parents can provide input

    D. All of the above

19. The definition of assistive technology devices was amended in the IDEA reauthorization of 2004 to exclude what?
    (Average)

    A. iPods and other hand-held devices

    B. Computer enhanced technology

    C. Surgically implanted devices

    D. Braille and/or special learning aids

20. The Individuals with Disabilities Education Act (IDEA) was signed into law in:
    (Average)

    A. 1975

    B. 1980

    C. 1990

    D. 1995

21. Section 504 differs from the scope of IDEA because its main focus is on:
    (Rigorous)

    A. Prohibition of discrimination on the basis of disability

    B. A basis for additional support services and accommodations in a special education setting

    C. Procedural rights and safeguards for the individual

    D. Federal funding for educational services

22. **Satisfaction of the Least Restrictive Environment (LRE) requirement means:**
    (Rigorous)

    A. The school is providing the best services it can offer

    B. The school is providing the best services the district has to offer

    C. The student is being educated with the fewest special education services necessary

    D. The student is being educated in the least restrictive setting that meets his or her needs

23. **What legislation started FAPE?**
    (Rigorous)

    A. Section 504

    B. EHCA

    C. IDEA

    D. Education Amendment 1974

24. **Which is untrue about the Americans with Disabilities Act (ADA)?**
    (Rigorous)

    A. It was signed into law the same year as IDEA by President Bush

    B. It reauthorized the discretionary programs of EHA

    C. It gives protection to all people on the basis of race, sex, national origin, and religion

    D. It guarantees equal opportunities to persons with disabilities in employment, public accommodations, transportation, government services, and telecommunications

25. **One of the most important goals of the special education teacher is to foster and create with the student:**
    (Easy)

    A. Handwriting skills

    B. Self-advocacy

    C. An increased level of reading

    D. Logical reasoning

26. **The best resource a teacher can have to reach a student is:**
    (Rigorous)

    A. Contact with the parents/guardians

    B. A successful behavior modification exam

    C. A listening ear

    D. Gathered scaffold approach to teaching

27. **The earliest establishment of organizations whose membership contained professionals in related fields serving individuals with disabilities came from:**
    (Rigorous)

    A. Sociology

    B. Psychology

    C. Medicine

    D. All of the Above

28. **The service medium facility that helps formerly institutionalized clients to adjust while becoming self-supporting members of the community is the:**
    (Rigorous)

    A. Half-way Residential Home

    B. Group Home

    C. Sheltered Workshop

    D. Foster Family Home

29. **Which is a less than ideal example of collaboration for successful inclusion?**
    (Average)

    A. Special education teachers are part of the instructional team in a regular classroom

    B. Special education teachers act as assistants to regular education teachers in the classroom

    C. Teaming approaches are used for problem solving and program implementation

    D. Regular teachers, special education teachers, and other specialists or support teachers co-teach

30. **The movement towards serving as many children with disabilities as possible in the regular classroom with supports and services grew out of:**
    (Average)

    A. The Full Service Model

    B. The Regular Education Model

    C. The Normalization movement

    D. The Mainstream Model

31. **Cognitive Learning strategies include:**
    (Rigorous)

    A. Reinforcing appropriate behavior

    B. Teaching students problem solving and critical thinking skills

    C. Heavily structuring the learning environment

    D. Generalizing learning from one setting to another

32. **Bob shows behavior problems such as lack of attention, getting out of his seat, and talking out. His teacher has kept data on these behaviors and has found that Bob is showing much better self-control since he has been self-managing himself through a behavior modification program. The most appropriate placement recommendation for Bob at this time is probably:**
    (Easy)

    A. Any available part-time special education program

    B. The regular classroom solely

    C. A behavior disorders resource room for one period a day

    D. A specific learning disabilities resource room for one period a day

33. **An important component of IDEA deals with "Due Process." Due Process is a set of procedures designed to ensure fairness and accountability in decisions related to the education of students with disabilities. Which of the following is NOT considered a Due Process right for parents under IDEA?**
    (Average)

    A. The right to specify which school personnel will work with their child

    B. The right to a Due Process Hearing if they do not agree with the school's recommendations

    C. The right to an Independent Educational Evaluation (IEE)

    D. The right to written notice prior to a prior to a proposal or refusal to initiate or make a change in the child's identification, evaluation, or educational placement

34. **The effective teacher varies her instructional presentations and response requirements depending upon:**
    (Easy)

    A. Student needs

    B. The task at hand

    C. The learning situation

    D. All of the above

35. The following words describe an IEP objective EXCEPT:
    (Average)

    A. Specific

    B. Observable

    C. Measurable

    D. Criterion-referenced

36. Which one of the following is NOT a primary purpose of an IEP?
    (Rigorous)

    A. To outline instructional programs

    B. To develop self-advocacy skills

    C. To function as the basis for evaluation

    D. To facilitate communication among staff members, teachers, parents, and students

37. _____ is a method used to increase student engaged learning time by having students teach other students.
    (Easy)

    A. Peer tutoring

    B. Engaged learning time

    C. Allocated learning time

    D. Teacher consultation

38. The Integrated approach to learning utilizes all resources available to address student needs. What are the resources?
    (Rigorous)

    A. The student, his/her parents, and the teacher

    B. The teacher, the parents, and the special education team

    C. The teacher, the student, and an administrator to perform needed interventions

    D. The student, his/her parents, the teacher, and community resources

39. Cooperative learning uses all these methods, EXCEPT:
    (Average)

    A. Shared ideas

    B. Small groups

    C. Independent practice

    D. Student expertise

40. **Presentation of tasks can be altered to match the student's rate of learning by:**
    (Rigorous)

    A. Describing how much of a topic is presented in one day, and how much practice is assigned, according to the student's abilities and learning style

    B. Using task analysis, assign a certain number of skills to be mastered in a specific amount of time

    C. Introducing a new task only when the student has demonstrated mastery of the previous task in the learning hierarchy

    D. A and C

41. **Alternative response patterns are educationally important because:**
    (Easy)

    A. They allow the special needs student the opportunity to approach a task from a position that best suits his learning style

    B. They permit the teacher to use her knowledge of the students' learning styles and capabilities to design the best learning environment for each student

    C. They allow all students, even non-readers, to interact in the instructional setting

    D. All of the above

42. **Which type of instructional arrangement established and enhances mutual respect for other students and promotes positive social goals:**
    (Rigorous)

    A. Homogeneous grouping

    B. One-on-one instruction

    C. Cooperative learning

    D. Small group instruction

43. **Functional skills include _____ skills.**
    (Easy)

    A. personal-social

    B. daily living

    C. occupational readiness

    D. All of the above

44. **In career education, specific training and preparation required for the world of work occurs during the phase of:**
    (Easy)

    A. Career Awareness

    B. Career Exploration

    C. Career Preparation

    D. Daily Living and Personal-Social Interaction

45. For which stage of learning would computer software be utilized that allows for continued drill and practice of a skill to achieve accuracy and speed?
(Average)

    A. Acquisition

    B. Proficiency

    C. Maintenance

    D. Generalization

46. When a student begins to use assistive technology, it is important for the teacher to have a clear outline as to when and how the equipment should be used. Why?
(Rigorous)

    A. To establish a level of accountability with the student

    B. To establish that the teacher has responsibility for the equipment that is in use in his/her room

    C. To establish that the teacher is responsible for the usage of the assistive technology

    D. To establish a guideline for evaluation

47. Which is characteristic of standardized group tests?
(Rigorous)

    A. Directions are always read to students

    B. The examiner monitors several students at the same time

    C. The teacher is allowed to probe students who almost have the correct answer

    D. Both quantitative and qualitative information may be gathered

48. Which of the following types of tests is used to estimate learning potential and to predict academic achievement?
(Easy)

    A. Intelligence Tests

    B. Achievement Tests

    C. Adaptive Behavior Tests

    D. Personality Tests

49. **In exceptional student education, assessment is used to make decisions about all of the following except:**
    (Average)

    A. Screening and initial identification of children who may need services

    B. Selection and evaluation of teaching strategies and programs

    C. Determining the desired attendance rate of a student

    D. Development of goals, objectives, and evaluation for the IEP

50. **Children who write poorly might be given tests that allow oral responses, unless the purpose for giving the test is to:**
    (Easy)

    A. Assess handwriting skills

    B. Test for organization of thoughts

    C. Answer questions pertaining to math reasoning

    D. Assess rote memory

51. **Alternative assessments include all of the following EXCEPT:**
    (Average)

    A. Portfolios

    B. Interviews

    C. Textbook chapter tests

    D. Student choice of assessment format

52. **According to Mercer and Mercer, what would be an appropriate amount of homework for a student in fourth grade:**
    (Average)

    A. 15 minutes, 3 days a week

    B. 45–75 minutes, 5 days a week

    C. 75–120 minutes, 5 days a week

    D. 15–45 minutes, 2 to 4 days a week

53. Mr. Brown finds that his chosen consequence does not seem to be having the desired effect of reducing the target misbehavior. Which of these would LEAST LIKELY account for Mr. Brown's lack of success with the consequence?
(Easy)

    A. The consequence was aversive in Mr. Brown's opinion but not the students'

    B. The students were not developmentally ready to understand the connection

    C. Mr. Brown was inconsistent in applying the consequence

    D. The intervention had not previously been shown to be effective in studies

54. When would proximity control not be a good behavioral intervention?
(Easy)

    A. Two students are arguing

    B. A student is distracting others

    C. One student threatens another

    D. Involve fading and shaping

55. Katie is frequently disruptive prior to each day's math lesson. From a behavior management perspective, the math lesson appears to be the _____ to Katie's undesirable disruptive behavior.
(Average)

    A. subsequent development

    B. succeeding force

    C. consequence

    D. antecedent

56. The best way to ensure the success of educational interventions is to:
(Average)

    A. Give regular education teachers the primary responsibility of teaching special needs students in regular classrooms

    B. Give special education teachers the primary responsibility of teaching special needs students in special education classrooms

    C. Promote cooperative teaching efforts between general and special educators

    D. Have support personnel assume the primary responsibility for the Education of special needs students

57. **In regard to the influence of teacher attitudes, which of the following is critical in the successful inclusion of the student with a disability:**
    (Average)

    A. The special education teacher should take full responsibility for the student with a disability

    B. The student with a disability only attend special events with the general education classroom

    C. Special education and regular education teachers should demonstrate the attitude that the exceptional student is a student of both teachers, not a special education student who only goes into a general education classroom at certain times

    D. The general education should wait for the special education teacher to be in the classroom before interacting with the student

58. **Which of the following would promote a good working relationship with a paraprofessional who has been assigned to your classroom?**
    (Average)

    A. Having the paraprofessional grade papers

    B. Telling the paraprofessional what you expect him/her to do

    C. Offering support to paraprofessionals by observing their work with students and offering feedback and suggestions

    D. Asking the paraprofessional to sit in the back of the room and only interact with students when you direct them

59. **Related service providers include all of the following EXCEPT:**
    (Average)

    A. General education teachers

    B. Speech and language therapists

    C. Occupational therapists

    D. Psychologists

60. In conducting a parent conference, the teacher should address each of the following EXCEPT:
(Easy)

   A. Provide samples of student work and other relevant information

   B. Focus on observable behaviors

   C. Offer suggestions for better parenting

   D. Be a good listener

61. A ruling pertaining to the use of evaluation procedures later consolidated in Public Law 94 – 142 resulted from which court case listed?
(Average)

   A. Diana v. the State Board of Education (1970)

   B. Wyatt v. Stickney

   C. Larry P. v. Riles

   D. PASE v. Hannon

62. Included in data brought to the attention of Congress regarding the evaluation procedures for education of students with disabilities was the fact that:
(Easy)

   A. There were a large number of children and youths with disabilities in the United States.

   B. Many children with disabilities were not receiving an appropriate education.

   C. Many parents of children with disabilities were forced to seek services outside of the public realm.

   D. All of the above

63. The Individuals with Disabilities Education Act (IDEA) was signed into law in and later reauthorized through a second revision in what years?
(Rigorous)

   A. 1975 and 2004

   B. 1980 and 1990

   C. 1990 and 2004

   D. 1995 and 2001

64. How was the training of special education teachers changed by the No Child Left Behind Act of 2002?
    (Rigorous)

    A. It required all special education teachers to be certified in reading and math.

    B. It required all special education teachers to take the same coursework as general education teachers.

    C. If a special education teacher is teaching a core subject, he or she must meet the standard of a highly-qualified teacher in that subject.

    D. All of the above

65. The No Child Left Behind Act (NCLB) affected students with Limited English Proficiency (LEP) by:
    (Rigorous)

    A. Requiring these students to demonstrate English Language Proficiency before a High School Diploma is granted.

    B. Providing allowances for schools not to require them to take and pass state Reading Exams (RCTs) if the students were enrolled in U.S. schools for less than a year.

    C. Providing allowances for these students to opt out of state math tests if the students were enrolled in a U.S. school for less than one year.

    D. Both B and C

66. Which of the following is a specific change of language in the IDEA?
    (Rigorous)

    A. The term "Disorder" changed to "Disability."

    B. The term "Children" changed to "Children and Youth."

    C. The term "Handicapped" changed to "Impairments."

    D. The term "Handicapped" changed to "With Disabilities."

19

67. Which component changed with the reauthorization of the Education for all Handicapped Children Act of 1975 (EHA) 1990 EHA Amendment?
    (Rigorous)

    A. Specific terminology

    B. Due process protections

    C. Non-discriminatory reevaluation procedures

    D. Individual education plans

68. Donna has been labeled "learning disabled" since second grade and has developed a fear of not being able to keep up with her peers. She has just entered middle school with a poor self-concept and often acts out to cover up her fear of failure. What is the most appropriate action her teacher can take when Donna exhibits minor inappropriate behavior?
    (Rigorous)

    A. Ignore the behavior unless it is too dangerous or distracting.

    B. Praise her for her correct behavior and responses.

    C. Discuss the inappropriate behavior tactfully and in private.

    D. All of the above.

69. Which of the following is the first step you should take to prepare to teach preparation for social situations?
    (Average)

    A. Allow students to plan events.

    B. Lecture.

    C. Anticipate possible problems.

    D. Take your students to the anticipated setting.

70. The opportunity for persons with disabilities to live as close to a normal life as possible describes:
    (Average)

    A. Least restrictive environment

    B. Normalization

    C. Mainstreaming

    D. Deinstitutionalization

71. **Requirements for evaluations were changed in IDEA 2004 to reflect that no 'single' assessment or measurement tool can be used to determine special education qualification, furthering that there was a disproportionate representation of what types of students?**
(Average)

    A. Disabled

    B. Foreign

    C. Gifted

    D. Minority and bilingual

72. **What determines whether a person is entitled to protection under Section 504?**
(Average)

    A. The individual must meet the definition of a person with a disability.

    B. The person must be able to meet the requirements of a particular program in spite of his or her disability.

    C. The school, business, or other facility must be the recipient of federal funding assistance.

    D. All of the above

73. **Legislation in Public Law 94 – 142 attempts to:**
(Rigorous)

    A. Match the child's educational needs with appropriate educational services.

    B. Include parents in the decisions made about their child's education.

    C. Establish a means by which parents can provide input.

    D. All of the above

74. **Effective transition was included in:**
(Rigorous)

    A. President Bush's 1990 State of the Union Message

    B. Public Law 101-476

    C. Public Law 95-207

    D. Both A and B

75. **The Free and Appropriate Public Education (FAPE) describes Special Education and related services as**
(Easy)

    A. Public expenditure and standard to the state educational agency.

    B. Provided in conformity with each student's individualized education program, if the program is developed to meet requirements of the law.

    C. Including preschool, elementary, and/or secondary education in the state involved.

    D. All of the above

76. **Jane is a third grader. Mrs. Smith, her teacher, noted that Jane was having difficulty with math and reading assignments. The results from recent diagnostic tests showed a strong sight vocabulary and strength in computational skills, but a weakness in comprehending what she read. This weakness was apparent in mathematical word problems as well. The multi-disciplinary team recommended placement in a special education resource room for learning disabilities two periods each school day. For the remainder of the school day, her placement will be:**
(Easy)

    A In the regular classroom

    B. At a special school

    C. In a self-contained classroom

    D. In a resource room for children with intellectual disabilities

77. Which of the following must be provided in a written notice to parents when proposing a child's educational placement?
(Average)

   A. A list of parental due process safeguards

   B. A list of current test scores

   C. A list of persons responsible for the child's education

   D. A list of academic subjects the child has passed

78. Zero Reject requires all children with disabilities be provided with what?
(Average)

   A. Total exclusion of functional exclusion

   B. Adherence to the annual local education agency (LEA) reporting

   C. Free, appropriate public education

   D. Both B and C

79. Students who receive special services in a regular classroom with consultation generally have academic and/or social-interpersonal performance deficits at which level of severity?
(Easy)

   A. Mild

   B. Moderate

   C. Severe

   D. Profound

80. The greatest number of students receiving special services is enrolled primarily in:
(Average)

   A. The regular classroom

   B. The resource room

   C. Self-contained classrooms

   D. Special schools

81. The most restrictive environment in which an individual might be placed and receive instruction is that of:
(Easy)

   A. Institutional setting

   B. Homebound instruction

   C. Special schools

   D. Self-contained special classes

82. The law affects required components of the IEP; elements required by the IEP and the law are:
(Rigorous)

    A. Present level of academic and functional performance; statement of how the disability affects the student's involvement and progress; evaluation criteria and timeliness for instructional objective achievement; modifications of accommodations

    B. Projected dates for services initiation with anticipated frequency, location and duration; statement of when parent will be notified; statement of annual goals

    C. Extent to which child will not participate in regular education program; transitional needs for students age 14.

    D. All of the above.

83. IEPs continue to have multiple sections; one section, present levels, now addresses what?
(Average)

    A. Academic achievement and functional performance

    B. English as a second language

    C. Functional performance

    D. Academic achievement

84. What is true about IDEA? In order to be eligible, a student must:
(Easy)

    A. Have a medical disability

    B. Have a disability that fits into one of the categories listed in the law

    C. Attend a private school

    D. Be a slow learner

85. Changes in requirements for Current Levels of Performance require:
(Average)

    A. Student voice in each Present Level of Performance.

    B. CSE chair must tell parents when child has unrealistic goals.

    C. Parent/Guardian must attend either by phone conference or in person.

    D. Teachers must write post-adult outcomes assigning a student to a specific field.

86. **Developmental Disabilities:**
    (Rigorous)

    A. Is the categorical name for intellectual disabilities in IDEA

    B. Includes congenital conditions, such as severe spina bifida, deafness, blindness, or profound intellectual disabilities

    C. Includes children who contract diseases, such as polio or meningitis, and who are left in an incapacitated functional state

    D. Both B and C

87. **Which of the following goals reflects new IDEA requirements?**
    (Rigorous)

    A. Janet wants to be a doctor.

    B. Frank plans to attend the Culinary Institute.

    C. Janet will go to college.

    D. Carmel currently lives independently (on her own).

88. **The definition for "Other Health Impaired (OHI)" in IDEA:**
    (Rigorous)

    A. Is the definition that accepts heart conditions

    B. Includes deafness, blindness, or profound intellectual disabilities

    C. Includes Autism and PDD

    D. Includes cochlear implants.

89. **Which is an educational characteristic common to students with mild intellectual learning and behavioral disabilities?**
    (Easy)

    A. Show interest in schoolwork

    B. Have intact listening skills

    C. Require modification in classroom instruction

    D. Respond better to passive than to active learning tasks

90. In general, characteristics of students with learning disabilities include:
(Average)

    A. A low level of performance in a majority of academic skill areas

    B. Limited cognitive ability

    C. A discrepancy between achievement and potential

    D. A uniform pattern of academic development

91. Michael's teacher complains that he is constantly out of his seat. She also reports that he has trouble paying attention to what is going on in class for more than a couple of minutes at a time. He appears to be trying, but his writing is often illegible, containing many reversals. Although he seems to want to please, he is very impulsive and stays in trouble with his teacher. He is failing reading, and his math grades, though somewhat better, are still below average. Michael's psychometric evaluation should include assessment for:
(Average)

    A. Mild intellectual disabilities

    B. Specific learning disabilities

    C. Mild behavior disorders

    D. Hearing impairment

92. Joey is in a mainstreamed preschool program. One of the means his teacher uses in determining growth in adaptive skills is that of observation. Some questions about Joey's behavior that she might ask include:
(Average)

    A. Is he able to hold a cup?

    B. Can he call the name of any of his toys?

    C. Can he reach for an object and grasp it?

    D. All of the above

93. Individuals with intellectual disabilities can be characterized as:
(Rigorous)

    A. Often indistinguishable from normal developing children at an early age

    B. Having a higher than normal rate of motor activity

    C. Displaying significant discrepancies in ability levels

    D. Uneducable in academic skills

94. **Which of the following statements is true about children with emotional/behavioral disorders?**
    (Average)

    A. They have very high IQs.

    B. They display poor social skills.

    C. They are poor academic achievers.

    D. Both B and C

95. **Which behavior would be expected at the mild level of emotional/behavioral disorders?**
    (Average)

    A. Attention seeking

    B. Inappropriate affect

    C. Self-Injurious

    D. Poor sense of identity

96. **Children with disabilities are LEAST likely to improve their social-interpersonal skills by:**
    (Rigorous)

    A. Developing sensitivity to other people

    B. Making behavioral choices in social situations

    C. Developing social maturity

    D. Talking with their sister or brother

97. **Autism is a condition characterized by:**
    (Easy)

    A. Distorted relationships with others

    B. Perceptual anomalies

    C. Self-stimulation

    D. All of the above

98. **As a separate exceptionality category in IDEA, autism:**
    (Average)

    A. Includes emotional/behavioral disorders as defined in federal regulations

    B. Adversely affects educational performance

    C. Is thought to be a form of mental illness

    D. Is a developmental disability that affects verbal and non-verbal communication

99. **Normality in child behavior is influenced by society's?**
    (Average)

    A. Attitudes and cultural beliefs

    B. Hereditary factors

    C. Prenatal care

    D. Attitudes and Victorian era motto

100. The CST coordinates and participates in due diligence through what process? *(Average)*

A. Child study team meets for the first time without parents.

B. Teachers take child learning concerns to the school counselor.

C. School counselor contacts parents for permission to perform screening assessments.

D. All of the above

101. Which of the following examples would be considered of highest priority when determining the need for the delivery of appropriate special education and related services? *(Rigorous)*

A. An eight-year-old boy is repeating first grade for the second time and exhibits problems with toileting, gross motor functions, and remembering number and letter symbols. His regular classroom teacher claims the referral forms are too time-consuming and refuses to complete them. He also refuses to make accommodations because he feels every child should be treated alike.

B. A six-year-old girl who has been diagnosed as autistic is placed in a special education class within the local school. Her mother wants her to attend residential school next year even though the girl is showing progress.

C. A ten-year-old girl with profound intellectual disabilities who is receiving education services in a state institution.

D. A twelve-year-old boy with mild disabilities who was placed in a behavior disorders program but displays obvious perceptual deficits (e.g., reversal of letters and symbols and inability to discriminate sounds). He originally was thought to have a learning disability but did not meet state criteria for this exceptionality category based on results of standard scores. He has always had problems with attending to a task and is now beginning to get into trouble during seatwork time. His teacher feels that he will eventually become a real behavior problem. He receives social skills training in the resource room one period a day.

102. **When a student is identified as being at-risk academically or socially what does Federal law hope for first?**
(Rigorous)

   A. Move the child quickly to assessment.

   B. Place the child in special education as soon as possible.

   C. Observe the child to determine what is wrong.

   D. Perform remedial intervention in the classroom.

103. **What do the 9th and 10th Amendments to the U.S. Constitution state about education?**
(Average)

   A. That education belongs to the people

   B. That education is an unstated power vested in the states

   C. That elected officials mandate education

   D. That education is free

104. **The IDEA states that child assessment is?**
(Average)

   A. At intervals with teacher discretion

   B. Continuous on a regular basis

   C. Left to the counselor

   D. Conducted annually

105. **Safeguards against bias and discrimination in the assessment of children include:**
(Average)

   A. The testing of a child in Standard English

   B. The requirement for the use of one standardized test

   C. The use of evaluative materials in the child's native language or other mode of communication

   D. All testing performed by a certified, licensed psychologist

106. Which is characteristic of group tests?
(Average)

A. Directions are always read to students.

B. The examiner monitors several students at the same time.

C. The teacher is allowed to probe students who almost have the correct answer.

D. Both quantitative and qualitative information may be gathered.

107. For which of the following uses are standardized individual tests MOST appropriate?
(Rigorous)

A. Screening students to determine possible need for special education services

B. Evaluation of special education curricula

C. Tracking of gifted students

D. Evaluation of a student for eligibility and placement, or individualized program planning, in special education

108. Which of the following is an advantage of giving informal individual rather than standardized group tests?
(Easy)

A. Questions can be modified to reveal a specific student's strategies or misconceptions.

B. The test administrator can clarify or rephrase questions.

C. They can be inserted into the class quickly on an as needed basis.

D. All of the above

109. Mrs. Stokes has been teaching her third grade students about mammals during a recent science unit. Which of the following would be true of a criterion-referenced test she might administer at the conclusion of the unit?
(Average)

A. It will be based on unit objectives.

B. Derived scores will be used to rank student achievement.

C. Standardized scores are effective of national performance samples.

D. All of the above

110. For which of the following purposes is a norm-referenced test LEAST appropriate?
(Rigorous)

   A. Screening

   B. Individual program planning

   C. Program evaluation

   D. Making placement decisions

111. Criterion-referenced tests can provide information about:
(Rigorous)

   A. Whether a student has mastered prerequisite skills

   B. Whether a student is ready to proceed to the next level of instruction

   C. Which instructional materials might be helpful in covering program objectives

   D. All of the above

112. Which of the following purposes of testing calls for an informal test?
(Average)

   A. Screening a group of children to determine their readiness for the first reader

   B. Analyzing the responses of a student with a disability to various presentations of content material to see which strategy works.

   C. Evaluating the effectiveness of a fourth-grade math program at the end of its first year of use in a specific school

   D. Determining the general level of intellectual functioning of a class of fifth graders

113. Which of the following is not a true statement about informal tests?
(Average)

   A. Informal tests are useful in comparing students to others of their age or grade level.

   B. The correlation between curriculum and test criteria is much higher in informal tests.

   C. Informal tests are useful in evaluating an individual's response to instruction.

   D. Informal tests are used to diagnose a student's particular strengths and weaknesses for purposes of planning individual programs.

114. **For which situation might a teacher be apt to select a formal test?**
(Rigorous)

   A. A pretest for studying world religions

   B. A weekly spelling test

   C. To compare student progress with that of peers of same age or grade level on a national basis

   D. To determine which content objectives outlined on the student's IEP were mastered

115. **The Key Math Diagnostic Arithmetic Test is an individually administered test of math skills. It is comprised of fourteen subtests, which are classified into the major math areas of content, operations, and applications for which subtest scores are reported. The test manual describes the population sample upon which the test was normed and reports data pertaining to reliability and validity. In addition, for each item in the test, a behavioral objective is presented. From the description, it can be determined that this achievement test is:**
(Rigorous)

   A. Individually administered

   B. Criterion-referenced

   C. Diagnostic

   D. All of the above

116. **The best measures of a student's functional capabilities and entry-level skills are:**
(Rigorous)

   A. Norm-referenced tests

   B. Teacher-made post-tests

   C. Standardized IQ tests

   D. Criterion-referenced measures

117. **One of your students receives a percentile rank of 45 on a standardized test. This indicates that the student's score:**
(Rigorous)

   A. Consisted of 45 correct answers

   B. Was at the point above which 45% of the other scores fell

   C. Was at the point below which 45% of the other scores fell

   D. Was below passing

118. **When you need to evaluate a student's work ethics, you should give what assessment?**
(Rigorous)

   A. Naturalistic

   B. Dynamic

   C. Performance-based

   D. Criterion-referenced

119. **Alternative assessments include all of the following EXCEPT:**
(Average)

   A. Portfolios

   B. Interviews

   C. Textbook chapter tests

   D. Student choice of assessment format

120. **Which of the following is an example of an alternative assessment?**
(Rigorous)

   A. Testing skills in a "real world" setting in several settings

   B. Pre-test of student knowledge of fractions before beginning wood shop

   C. Answering an essay question that allows for creative thought

   D. A compilation of a series of tests in a portfolio

Praxis Special Education Practice Test Kit
Pre-Test Sample Questions with Rationales

1. All of the following EXCEPT one are characteristics of a student who is Emotionally Disturbed:
   (Average)

   A. Socially accepted by peers

   B. Highly disruptive to the classroom environment

   C. Academic difficulties

   D. Areas of talent overlooked by a teacher

Answer: A. Socially accepted by peers
While a such a child **may** be socially accepted by peers, children who are emotionally disturbed tend to alienate those around them and are often ostracized.

2. Which of these characteristics is NOT included in the IDEA definition of emotional disturbance?
   (Rigorous)

   A. General pervasive mood of unhappiness or depression

   B. Social maladjustment manifested in a number of settings

   C. Tendency to develop physical symptoms, pains, or fear associated with school or personal problems

   D. Inability to learn that is not attributed to intellectual, sensory, or health factors

Answer: B. Social maladjustment manifested in a number of settings
Social maladjustment is not considered a disability.

3. **Truancy, gang membership, and a feeling of pride in belonging to a delinquent subculture are indicative of:**
   (Average)

   A. Conduct disorder

   B. Personality disorders

   C. Immaturity

   D. Socialized aggression

Answer: D. Socialized aggression
The student is acting out by using aggression. This gives him a sense of belonging.

4. **Indirect requests and attempts to influence or control others through one's use of language is an example of:**
   (Rigorous)

   A. Morphology

   B. Syntax

   C. Pragmatics

   D. Semantics

Answer: C. Pragmatics
Pragmatics involves the way that language is used to communicate and interact with others. It is often used to control the actions and attitudes of other people.

5. Scott is in middle school but still makes statements like, "I gotted new high-tops yesterday," and "I saw three mans in the front office." Language interventions for Scott would target:
   (Average)

   A. Morphology

   B. Syntax

   C. Pragmatics

   D. Semantics

Answer A. Morphology
Students with problems in this area may not use inflectional endings in their words, may not be consistent in their use of certain morphemes, or may be delayed in learning such morphemes as irregular past tenses.

6. Which component of language involves language content rather than the form of language?
   (Rigorous)

   A. Phonology

   B. Morphology

   C. Semantics

   D. Syntax

Answer: C. Semantics
Semantics is the study of the relationships between words and grammatical forms in a language, and their underlying meaning: the content, rather than the form of language

7. **Which of the following characteristics is probably most related to physical impairments?**
   (Rigorous)

   A. Lack of physical stamina

   B. Progressive weakening of muscles

   C. Impaired motor abilities

   D. Side effects from treatment

Answer: C. Impaired motor abilities
The other three conditions may exist in persons with other disabilities. Generally, children with physical disabilities display a variety of conditions. Each condition primarily affects one particular system of the body:

- The cardiopulmonary system affects the blood vessels, heart and lungs.
- The musculoskeletal system affects the muscles, bones and joints.
- The neurological system affects the spinal cord, brain and nerves.

Some conditions develop during pregnancy, at birth, or during infancy, due to factors known and unknown. Others occur later due to disease, injury trauma, or other factors. Besides motor disorders, individuals with physical disabilities may also have multi-disabling conditions like concomitant hearing impairments, visual impairments, perceptual disorders, speech defects, behavior disorders, or mental handicaps. Neurological impairments may also affect sensory abilities, cognitive functions, motor performance, and emotional responsiveness.

8. **Jennifer is eight years old and has been diagnosed with intellectual disabilities. She exhibits the following characteristics: poor motor development, minimal speech and communication, is not potty trained, and requires constant supervision. How would she be classified in terms of degree of cognitive impairment?**
(Rigorous)

   A. Mild

   B. Moderate

   C. Severe

   D. Profound

Answer: C. Severe
Jennifer would most likely fall into the severe category. All categories are as follows:

Mild (IQ of 50–55 to 70)
- Delays in most areas (communication, motor, academic)
- Often not distinguished from normal children until of school age.
- Can acquire both academic and vocational skills; can become self-supporting

Moderate (IQ of 35–40 to 50–55)
- Only fair motor development; clumsy
- Poor social awareness
- Can be taught to communicate
- Can profit from training in social and vocational skills; needs supervision, but can perform semiskilled labor as an adult

Severe (IQ of 20–25 to 35–40)
- Poor motor development
- Minimal speech and communication
- Minimal ability to profit from training in health and self-help skills: may contribute to self-maintenance under constant supervision as an adult

Profound (IQ below 20–25)
- Gross retardation, both mental and sensor-motor
- Little or no development of basic communication skills
- Dependency on others to maintain basic life functions
- Lifetime of complete supervision (institution, home, nursing home)

9. Otumba is a 16 year old in your class who recently came from Nigeria. The girls in your class have come to you to complain about the way he treats them in a sexist manner. When they complain you reflect that this is also the way he treats adult females. You have talked to Otumba before about appropriate behavior. You should first:
   (Rigorous)

   A. Complain to the Principal

   B. Ask for a Parent-Teacher Conference

   C. Check to see if this is a cultural norm in his country

   D. Create a behavior contract for him to follow

Answer: C. Check to see if this is a cultural norm in his country
While choices A, B, and D are appropriate actions, it is important to remember that Otumba comes from a culture where woman are treated differently than they are here in America. Learning this information will enable the school as a whole to address this behavior.

10. Some of the factors that can contribute to learning disabilities and/or cognitive impairments include problems with fetal brain development, genetic factors, environmental factors, problems during pregnancy or delivery, environmental toxins, and the use of drugs or alcohol during pregnancy. Which of the following conditions can be directly related to one of the above listed factors?
    (Easy)

    A. Emotional Disturbance

    B. Fetal Alcohol Syndrome

    C. Learning Disability

    D. Attention Deficit Disorder

Answer: B. Fetal Alcohol Syndrome
Heavy alcohol use during pregnancy has been linked to Fetal Alcohol Syndrome (FAS), a condition resulting in low birth weight, intellectual impairment, hyperactivity, and certain physical defects.

11. **Statements like, "Darren is lazy," are not helpful in describing his behavior for all but which of these reasons?**
    (Rigorous)

    A. There is no way to determine if any change occurs from the information given

    B. The student and not the behavior becomes labeled

    C. Darren's behavior will manifest itself clearly enough without any written description

    D. Such labels are open to various interpretations among the people who are asked to define them

Answer: C. Darren's behavior will manifest itself clearly enough without any written description

"Darren is lazy" is a label. It can be interpreted in a variety of ways, and there is no way to measure this description for change. A description should be measurable. In addition, this label focuses upon the child, not the behavior to be assessed.

12. **Criteria for choosing behaviors that most need change involve all but the following:**
    (Average)

    A. Observations across settings to rule out certain interventions

    B. Pinpointing the behavior that is the poorest fit in the child's environment

    C. The teacher's concern about what is the most important behavior to target

    D. Analysis of the environmental reinforcers

Answer: C. The teacher's concern about what is the most important behavior to target

Choices A, B, and D are more objective measures of the behavior and its effects. As such, it is these that should be the focus of the teacher's efforts. The teacher should focus her/his concern on objective measures of behavior.

13. **Measuring frequency is appropriate for all of these behaviors EXCEPT:**
    (Rigorous)

    A. Teasing

    B. Talking out

    C. Being on time for class

    D. Off-task behavior

Answer: D. Off-task behavior
Off-task behavior is relevant because it reduces time on task or engaged learning time. Therefore, it is better measured by duration.

14. **Which is generally true about students with mild disabilities?**
    (Easy)

    A. Comprise about half of the total special education population

    B. Are generally recognized once they begin school and have learning challenges

    C. Have a high school dropout rate

    D. All of the above

Answer: D. All of the above
This population is no different physically from other students, so their disabilities may not be noticed until the requirements of school begin. They do drop out of school at a higher rate than the non-disabled students do, and they comprise about half of the population of students with disabilities.

15. **Which of the following is true about autism?**
    (Rigorous)

    A. It is caused by having cold, aloof or hostile parents

    B. Approximately 4 out of 10 people have autism

    C. It is a Separate Exceptionality Category in IDEA

    D. It is a form of Mental Illness

Answer: C. It is a Separate Exceptionality Category in IDEA
Smith and Luckasson (1992) describe autism as a severe language disorder that affects thinking, communication, and behavior. They list the following characteristics:

- **Absent or distorted relationships with people**—inability to relate with people except as objects, inability to express affection, or ability to build and maintain only distant, suspicious or bizarre relationships.
- **Extreme or peculiar problems in communication**—absence of verbal language or language that is not functional, such as echolalia (parroting what one hears), misuse of pronouns (e.g. he for you or I for her), neologisms (made-up meaningless words or sentences), talk that bears little or no resemblance to reality.
- **Self-stimulation**—repetitive stereotyped behavior that seems to have no purpose other than providing sensory stimulation. This may take a wide variety of forms, such as swishing saliva, twirling objects, patting one's cheeks, flapping one's arms, staring, etc.
- **Self-injury**—repeated physical self-abuse, such as biting, scratching, or poking oneself, head banging, etc.
- **Perceptual anomalies**—unusual responses or absence of response to stimuli that seem to indicate sensory impairment or unusual sensitivity.

16. **In which of the following exceptionality categories may a student be considered for inclusion if his IQ score falls more than two standard deviations below the mean?**
    (Average)

    A. Intellectual disabilities

    B. Specific Learning Disabilities

    C. Emotionally/Behaviorally Disordered

    D. Gifted

Answer: A. Intellectual disabilities
Only about 1 to 1.5% of the population fit the AAMD's definition of intellectual disabilities. They fall outside the 2 standard deviations limit for Special Learning Disabilities and Emotionally/Behaviorally disordered.

17. **According to IDEA, a child whose disability is related to being deaf and blind may not be classified as:**
    (Rigorous)

    A. Multiple Disabilities

    B. Other Health Impaired

    C. Mentally Retarded

    D. Visually Impaired

Answer: A. Multiple Disabilities
The only stated area where deaf-blindness is not accepted is in Multiple Disabilities. Deaf-blind is a separate category on the IDEA classification list, so inclusion in Multiple Disabilities would be redundant.

18. **Legislation in Public Law 94 – 142 attempts to:**
    (Average)

    A. Match the child's educational needs with appropriate educational services

    B. Include parents in the decisions made about their child's education

    C. Establish a means by which parents can provide input

    D. All of the above

Answer: D. All of the above

Much of what was stated in separate court rulings and mandated legislation was brought together into what is now considered to be the "backbone" of special education. Public Law 94 – 142 (Education for All Handicapped Children Act) was signed into law by President Ford in 1975. It was the culmination of a great deal of litigation and legislation from the late 1960s to the mid-1970s, which included decisions supporting the need to assure an appropriate education to all persons regardless of race, creed, or disability.

In 1990, this law was reauthorized and renamed the Individuals with Disabilities Education Act, IDEA.

19. **The definition of assistive technology devices was amended in the IDEA reauthorization of 2004 to exclude what?**
    (Average)

    A. iPods and other hand-held devices

    B. Computer enhanced technology

    C. Surgically implanted devices

    D. Braille and/or special learning aids

Answer: C. Surgically implanted devices
The definition of assistive technology devices was amended to exclude devices that are surgically implanted (i.e. cochlear implants), and it clarified that students with assistive technology devices shall not be prevented from having special education services. Assistive technology devices may need to be monitored by school personnel, but schools are not responsible for the surgical implantation or replacement of such devices.

20. **The Individuals with Disabilities Education Act (IDEA) was signed into law in:**
    (Average)

    A. 1975

    B. 1980

    C. 1990

    D. 1995

Answer: C. 1990
IDEA, Public Law 101 – 476 is a consolidation and reauthorization of all prior Special Education mandates, with amendments. It was signed into law by President Bush on October 30, 1990.

21. **Section 504 differs from the scope of IDEA because its main focus is on:**
    (Rigorous)

    A. Prohibition of discrimination on the basis of disability

    B. A basis for additional support services and accommodations in a special education setting

    C. Procedural rights and safeguards for the individual

    D. Federal funding for educational services

Answer: A. Prohibition of discrimination on the basis of disability
Section 504 prohibits discrimination on the basis of disability.

22. **Satisfaction of the Least Restrictive Environment (LRE) requirement means:**
    (Rigorous)

    A. The school is providing the best services it can offer

    B. The school is providing the best services the district has to offer

    C. The student is being educated with the fewest special education services necessary

    D. The student is being educated in the least restrictive setting that meets his or her needs

Answer: D. The student is being educated in the least restrictive setting that meets his or her needs
The legislation mandates LRE. Exactly what constitutes LRE for a given child will depend upon his or her individual needs.

23. **What legislation started FAPE?**
    (Rigorous)

    A.   Section 504

    B.   EHCA

    C.   IDEA

    D.   Education Amendment 1974

Answer: A. Section 504
FAPE stands for Free Appropriate Public Education. Section 504 of the Rehabilitation Act in 1973 is the legislation that enacted FAPE. Since that time, it has been expanded and reauthorized in various forms of IDEA (Individuals with Disabilities Education Act).

24. **Which is untrue about the Americans with disabilities Act (ADA)?**
    (Rigorous)

    A.   It was signed into law the same year as IDEA by President Bush

    B.   It reauthorized the discretionary programs of EHA

    C.   It gives protection to all people on the basis of race, sex, national origin, and religion

    D.   It guarantees equal opportunities to persons with disabilities in employment, public accommodations, transportation, government services, and telecommunications

Answer: B. It reauthorized the discretionary programs of EHA
EHA is the precursor of IDEA, the Individuals with Disabilities Education Act. ADA, however, is Public Law 101 – 336, the Americans with Disabilities Act, which gives civil rights protection to all individuals with disabilities in private sector employment, all public services, public accommodations, transportation, and telecommunications. It was patterned after the Rehabilitation Act of 1973.

25. **One of the most important goals of the special education teacher is to foster and create with the student:**
    (Easy)

    A. Handwriting skills

    B. Self-advocacy

    C. An increased level of reading

    D. Logical reasoning

Answer: B. Self-advocacy
When a student achieves the ability to recognize his/her deficits and knows how to correctly advocate for his/her needs, the child has learned one of the most important life skills.

26. **The best resource a teacher can have to reach a student is:**
    (Rigorous)

    A. Contact with the parents/guardians

    B. A successful behavior modification exam

    C. A listening ear

    D. Gathered scaffold approach to teaching

Answer: A. Contact with the parents/guardians
Parents are often the best source of information on their children. They generally know if a behavior management technique will be successful.

27. **The earliest establishment of organizations whose membership contained professionals in related fields serving individuals with disabilities came from:**
(Rigorous)

    A.   Sociology

    B.   Psychology

    C.   Medicine

    D.   All of the Above

Answer: B. Psychology
The American Psychological Association (APA) is a scientific and professional society working to improve mental health services and to advocate for legislation and programs that will promote mental health; facilitate research, and professional development. It was founded at Clark University in 1892 for the advancement of psychology as a science. The association was incorporated in 1925 in Washington, D.C. Some of the early professionals responsible for serving individuals with disabilities are Thomas Hopkins Galludet, Samuel Gridley, Edward Seguin, Louis Terman, Maria Montessori, John B. Watson, and B. F. Skinner.

28. **The service medium facility that helps formerly institutionalized clients to adjust while becoming self-supporting members of the community is the:** *(Rigorous)*

    A.   Half-way Residential Home

    B.   Group Home

    C.   Sheltered Workshop

    D.   Foster Family Home

Answer: A. Half-way Residential Home
Half-way residential houses are available in some communities for formerly institutionalized individuals who need support while receiving vocational training and learning to be more independent. These may offer other forms of support, such as daily living skills and social/interpersonal counseling.

29. **Which is a less than ideal example of collaboration for successful inclusion?**
(Average)

   A. Special education teachers are part of the instructional team in a regular classroom

   B. Special education teachers act as assistants to regular education teachers in the classroom

   C. Teaming approaches are used for problem solving and program implementation

   D. Regular teachers, special education teachers, and other specialists or support teachers co-teach

Answer: B. Special education teachers act as assistants to regular education teachers in the classroom
Regular education teachers, special education teachers, and other specialists should work collaboratively to provide the best services to the student. Special education teachers should be more than just "assistants" in the regular classroom.

30. **The movement towards serving as many children with disabilities as possible in the regular classroom with supports and services grew out of:**
(Average)

   A. The Full Service Model

   B. The Regular Education Model

   C. The Normalization movement

   D. The Mainstream Model

Answer: C. The Normalization movement
The Normalization Movement advocated movement toward less restrictive environments for people with disabilities. It led to deinstitutionalization and the attempt to let people with disabilities live, go to school, and work in an environment as "normal," or as close as possible to that of their peer group without disabilities.

31. **Cognitive Learning strategies include:**
    (Rigorous)

    A. Reinforcing appropriate behavior

    B. Teaching students problem solving and critical thinking skills

    C. Heavily structuring the learning environment

    D. Generalizing learning from one setting to another

Answer: B. Teaching students problem solving and critical thinking skills
The Cognitive Learning approach to special education emphasizes measurable outcomes of a student's learning. It is often associated with Bloom's taxonomy of higher level thinking (knowledge, comprehension, application, analysis, and synthesis) and Haladyna's learning processes of understanding, problem solving, critical thinking, and creativity.

32. **Bob shows behavior problems such as lack of attention, out of seat, and talking out. His teacher has kept data on these behaviors and has found that Bob is showing much better self-control since he has been self-managing himself through a behavior modification program. The most appropriate placement recommendation for Bob at this time is probably:**
    (Easy)

    A. Any available part-time special education program

    B. The regular classroom solely

    C. A behavior disorders resource room for one period a day

    D. A specific learning disabilities resource room for one period a day

Answer: B. The regular classroom solely
Bob is able to self-manage himself and is very likely to behave like the other children in the regular classroom. The regular classroom is the least restrictive environment.

33. An important component of IDEA deals with "Due Process." Due Process a set of procedures designed to ensure fairness and accountability in decisions related to the education of students with disabilities. Which of the following is NOT considered a Due Process right for parents under IDEA?
    (Average)

    A.   The right to specify which school personnel will work with their child

    B.   The right to a Due Process Hearing if they do not agree with the school's recommendations

    C.   The right to an Independent Educational Evaluation (IEE)

    D.   The right to written notice prior to a prior to a proposal or refusal to initiate or make a change in the child's identification, evaluation, or educational placement

Answer: A. The right to specify which school personnel will work with their child
Assignment of school personnel remains the responsibility of the individual school and is not a component of Due Process according to IDEA.

34. The effective teacher varies her instructional presentations and response requirements depending upon:
    (Easy)

    A.   Student needs

    B.   The task at hand

    C.   The learning situation

    D.   All of the above

Answer: D. All of the above
Differentiated instruction and meeting the needs of the group as a whole must address the students' modes of learning to be successful.

35. The following words describe an IEP objective EXCEPT:
(Average)

    A.   Specific

    B.   Observable

    C.   Measurable

    D.   Criterion-referenced

Answer: D. Criterion-referenced
An Individual Education Plan (IEP) should be specific, observable, and measurable. Criterion referenced is a term used to define a type of test or assessment.

36. Which one of the following is NOT a primary purpose of an IEP?
(Rigorous)

    A.   To outline instructional programs

    B.   To develop self-advocacy skills

    C.   To function as the basis for evaluation

    D.   To facilitate communication among staff members, teachers, parents, and students

Answer: B. To develop self-advocacy skills
While self-advocacy should be encouraged, it is not one of the primary purposes of an IEP. It might, of course, be one of the goals listed for a child, if the IEP team feels it is important to their educational success.

37. _____ is a method used to increase student engaged learning time by having students teach other students.
(Easy)

   A.   Peer tutoring

   B.   Engaged learning time

   C.   Allocated learning time

   D.   Teacher consultation

Answer: A. Peer tutoring
Peer tutoring is a method for increasing student learning time by having students teach other students. Special care must be taken to be sure students are trained to use this method effectively and without one student feeling superior to another.

38. The Integrated approach to learning utilizes all resources available to address student needs. What are the resources?
(Rigorous)

   A.   The student, his/her parents, and the teacher.

   B.   The teacher, the parents, and the special education team.

   C.   The teacher, the student, and an administrator to perform needed interventions.

   D.   The student, his/her parents, the teacher, and community resources.

Answer: D. The student, his/her parents, the teacher, and community resources.
The integrated response encompasses all possible resources including the resources in the community.

39. Cooperative learning uses all these methods, EXCEPT:
(Average)

- A. Shared ideas
- B. Small groups
- C. Independent practice
- D. Student expertise

Answer: C. Independent practice
Cooperative learning focuses on group cooperation allowing for sharing of student expertise and provides some flexibility for creative presentation of the students as they share with others.

40. Presentation of tasks can be altered to match the student's rate of learning by:
(Rigorous)

- A. Describing how much of a topic is presented in one day, and how much practice is assigned, according to the student's abilities and learning style
- B. Using task analysis, assign a certain number of skills to be mastered in a specific amount of time
- C. Introducing a new task only when the student has demonstrated mastery of the previous task in the learning hierarchy
- D. A and C

Answer: D. A and C
Pacing is the term used for altering of tasks to match the student's rate of learning. This can be done in two ways: altering the subject content and the rate at which tasks are presented.

41. Alternative response patterns are educationally important because:
(Easy)

- A. They allow the special needs student the opportunity to approach a task from a position that best suits his learning style

- B. They permit the teacher to use her knowledge of the students' learning styles and capabilities to design the best learning environment for each student

- C. They allow all students, even non-readers, to interact in the instructional setting

- D. All of the above

Answer: D. All of the above

Instructional alternatives to help students with learning problems may be referred to as compensatory techniques, instructional adaptations, or accommodation techniques. Certain students have difficulty with writing answers but may be able to express their knowledge of subject matter verbally. Therefore, modifications of content area material may be extended to methods and modifications for evaluation and assessment of student progress. Teachers are learning the value of giving assignments that meet the individual abilities and needs of students. After instruction, discussion, questioning, and practice have been provided, rather than assigning one task to all students, teachers are asking students to generate tasks that will show their knowledge of the information presented. Students are given choices and thereby have the opportunity to demonstrate more effectively the skills, concepts, or topics that they as individuals have learned. It has been established that student choice increases student originality, intrinsic motivation, and higher mental processes.

42. **Which type of instructional arrangement established and enhances mutual respect for other students and promotes positive social goals:**
    (Rigorous)

    A. Homogeneous grouping

    B. One-on-one instruction

    C. Cooperative learning

    D. Small group instruction

Answer: C. Cooperative learning
Cooperative learning techniques can be used to establish and enhance mutual respect for other students. Cooperative learning can promote positive social goals when used effectively as a teaching and learning tool. When the teacher promotes interaction of students among ethnic and social groups, students tend to respond positively by forming friendships and having enhanced respect for other sociological groups. Thus, the teacher who effectively manages cooperative learning groups has not only promoted cognitive learning but has also promoted desirable behaviors in terms of mutual respect for all students.

43. **Functional skills include _____ skills.**
    (Easy)

    A. personal-social

    B. daily living

    C. occupational readiness

    D. All of the above

Answer: D. All of the above
A transition or vocational curriculum approach focuses upon what students need to learn that will be useful to them and prepare them for functioning in society as adults. Life preparation includes not only occupational readiness but also personal-social and daily living skills.

44. In career education, specific training and preparation required for the world of work occurs during the phase of:
(Easy)

   A. Career Awareness

   B. Career Exploration

   C. Career Preparation

   D. Daily Living and Personal-Social Interaction

Answer: C. Career Preparation
Curricular aspects of career education include:

- Career Awareness: diversity of available jobs
- Career Exploration: skills needed for occupational groups
- Career Preparation: specific training and preparation required for the world of work

45. For which stage of learning would computer software be utilized that allows for continued drill and practice of a skill to achieve accuracy and speed?
(Average)

   A. Acquisition

   B. Proficiency

   C. Maintenance

   D. Generalization

Answer: B. Proficiency
The definitions for the above terms are:

- **Acquisition**—Introduction of a new skill.
- **Maintenance**—Continued practice without further instruction.
- **Proficiency**—Practice under supervision to achieve accuracy and speed.
- **Generalization**—Application of the new skills in new settings and situations.

46. **When a student begins to use assistive technology, it is important for the teacher to have a clear outline as to when and how the equipment should be used. Why?**
    (Rigorous)

    A. To establish a level of accountability with the student

    B. To establish that the teacher has responsibility for the equipment that is in use in his/her room

    C. To establish that the teacher is responsible for the usage of the assistive technology

    D. To establish a guideline for evaluation

Answer: A. To establish a level of accountability with the student
Clear parameters as to the usage of assistive technology in a classroom create a level of accountability in the student. Both the student and the teacher should know the intended purpose and appropriate manner of use of the device.

47. **Which is characteristic of standardized group tests?**
    (Rigorous)

    A. Directions are always read to students

    B. The examiner monitors several students at the same time

    C. The teacher is allowed to probe students who almost have the correct answer

    D. Both quantitative and qualitative information may be gathered

Answer: B. The examiner monitors several students at the same time
In standardized group tests, directions and procedures are carefully prescribed and scripted. Children write or mark their own responses. The examiner monitors the progress of several children at the same time. He cannot rephrase questions or probe or prompt responses. It is very difficult to obtain qualitative information from standardized group tests. Standardized group tests are appropriate for program evaluation, screening, and some types of program planning, such as tracking. Special consideration may need to be given if there are any motivational, personality, linguistic, or physically disabling factors that might impair the examinee's performance. When planning individual programs, individual tests should be used.

48. Which of the following types of tests is used to estimate learning potential and to predict academic achievement?
    (Easy)

    A. Intelligence Tests

    B. Achievement Tests

    C. Adaptive Behavior Tests

    D. Personality Tests

Answer: A. Intelligence Tests
An intelligence test is designed to measure intellectual abilities like memory, comprehension, and abstract reasoning. IQ is often used to estimate the learning capacity of a student as well as to predict academic achievement.

49. In exceptional student education, assessment is used to make decisions about all of the following except:
    (Average)

    A. Screening and initial identification of children who may need services

    B. Selection and evaluation of teaching strategies and programs

    C. Determining the desired attendance rate of a student

    D. Development of goals, objectives, and evaluation for the IEP

Answer: C. Determining the desired attendance rate of a student
School attendance is required, and assessment is not necessary to measure a child's attendance rate.

50. Children who write poorly might be given tests that allow oral responses, unless the purpose for giving the test is to:
(Easy)

- A. Assess handwriting skills
- B. Test for organization of thoughts
- C. Answer questions pertaining to math reasoning
- D. Assess rote memory

Answer: A. Assess handwriting skills
It is necessary to have the child write if we are assessing their skill in that domain.

51. Alternative assessments include all of the following EXCEPT:
(Average)

- A. Portfolios
- B. Interviews
- C. Textbook chapter tests
- D. Student choice of assessment format

Answer: C. Textbook chapter tests
Textbook chapter tests are formal, usually multiple choice tests with one fixed, correct answer. Choices A, B, and D are alternative methods of assessment.

52. According to Mercer and Mercer, what would be an appropriate amount of homework for a student in fourth grade:
(Average)

    A.   15 minutes, 3 days a week

    B.   45–75 minutes, 5 days a week

    C.   75–120 minutes, 5 days a week

    D.   15–45 minutes, 2 to 4 days a week

Answer: D. 15–45 minutes, 2 to 4 days a week
The following are recommended times for students in regular education classes:

- **Primary Grades**—three 15-minutes assignments per week
- **Grades 4 to 6**—two to four 15 to 45-minute assignments per week
- **Grades 7 to 9**—as many as five 45 to 75-minute assignments per week
- **Grades 10 to 12**—as many as five 75 to 120 minute assignments per week

Homework assignments may need to be modified for some students with disabilities. Some students with disabilities may be unable to handle the usual amount of homework. Care should be taken to ensure that the homework practice is *practice*, not new learning. Like many aspects of instruction, homework should be differentiated.

53. **Mr. Brown finds that his chosen consequence does not seem to be having the desired effect of reducing the target misbehavior. Which of these would LEAST LIKELY account for Mr. Brown's lack of success with the consequence?**
(Easy)

   A.   The consequence was aversive in Mr. Brown's opinion but not the students'

   B.   The students were not developmentally ready to understand the connection

   C.   Mr. Brown was inconsistent in applying the consequence

   D.   The intervention had not previously been shown to be effective in studies

Answer: D. The intervention had not previously been shown to be effective in studies
Choices A, B, and C might work if applied in the classroom, but research is less relevant in this situation than the specific elements of Mr. Brown's class.

54. **When would proximity control not be a good behavioral intervention?**
(Easy)

   A.   Two students are arguing

   B.   A student is distracting others

   C.   One student threatens another

   D.   Involve fading and shaping

Answer: C. One student threatens another
Threats can break into fights. Standing in the middle of a fight can be threatening to your ability to supervise the class as a whole or to get the help needed to stop the fight.

55. **Katie frequently is disruptive prior to each day's math lesson. From a behavior management perspective, the math lesson appears to be the _____ to Katie's undesirable disruptive behavior.**
(Average)

    A. subsequent development

    B. succeeding force

    C. consequence

    D. antecedent

Answer: D. antecedent
Antecedents are the causes of behaviors, and they therefore precede the behavior. The special educator should be aware of antecedents to undesirable behaviors. These may include a time of day, a particular activity, a location, or a combination of people. While some upsetting situations may be avoided, it is often important to work with the student so that the situation is more tolerable.

56. **The best way to ensure the success of educational interventions is to:**
(Average)

    A. Give regular education teachers the primary responsibility of teaching special needs students in regular classrooms

    B. Give special education teachers the primary responsibility of teaching special needs students in special education classrooms

    C. Promote cooperative teaching efforts between general and special educators

    D. Have support personnel assume the primary responsibility for the education of special needs students

Answer: C. Promote cooperative teaching efforts between general and special educators
Both types of teachers can learn from each other, and students can learn from each other and become sensitive to the special needs of each other.

57. **In regard to the influence of teacher attitudes, which of the following is critical in the successful inclusion of the student with a disability:** *(Average)*

    A. The special education teacher should take full responsibility for the student with a disability

    B. The student with a disability only attend special events with the general education classroom

    C. Special education and regular education teachers should demonstrate the attitude that the exceptional student is a student of both teachers, not a special education student who only goes into a general education classroom at certain times

    D. The general education should wait for the special education teacher to be in the classroom before interacting with the student

Answer: C. Special education and regular education teachers should demonstrate the attitude that the exceptional student is a student of both teachers, not a special education student who only goes into a general education classroom at certain times
One of the key factors in successful inclusion is the attitude that the student is a true member of the classroom and a student of both teachers.

58. **Which of the following would promote a good working relationship with a paraprofessional who has been assigned to your classroom?** *(Average)*

    A. Having the paraprofessional grade papers

    B. Telling the paraprofessional what you expect him/her to do

    C. Offering support to paraprofessionals by observing their work with students and offering feedback and suggestions

    D. Asking the paraprofessional to sit in the back of the room and only interact with students when you direct them.

Answer: C. Offering support to paraprofessionals by observing their work with students and offering feedback and suggestions

CEC suggests that teachers can best collaborate with general education teachers and paraprofessionals by:

- Offering information about the characteristics and needs of children with exceptional learning needs
- Discussing and brainstorming ways to integrate children with exceptionalities into various settings within the school community
- Modeling best practices and instructional techniques and accommodations and coaching others in their use
- Keeping communication about children with exceptional learning needs and their families confidential
- Consulting with these colleagues in the assessment of individuals with exceptional learning needs
- Engaging them in group problem-solving and in developing, executing, and assessing collaborative activities
- Offering support to paraprofessionals by observing their work with students and offering feedback and suggestions

59. **Related service providers include all of the following EXCEPT:**
    (Average)

    A.   General education teachers

    B.   Speech and language therapists

    C.   Occupational therapists

    D.   Psychologists

Answer: A. General education teachers
General education teachers are important collaborators with teachers of exceptional students; however, they are not related service providers. Related service providers offer specialized skills and abilities that are critical to an exceptional education teacher's ability to advocate for his or her student and meet a school's legal obligations to the student and his or her family. Related service providers, such as speech, occupational, and language therapists and psychologists, offer expertise and resources unparalleled in meeting a child's developmental needs.

60. **In conducting a parent conference, the teacher should address each of the following EXCEPT:**
    (Easy)

    A.   Provide samples of student work and other relevant information

    B.   Focus on observable behaviors

    C.   Offer suggestions for better parenting

    D.   Be a good listener

Answer: C. Offer suggestions for better parenting
As you address issues or areas of concern, be sure to focus on observable behaviors and concrete results or information. Do not make judgmental statements about parent or child. Share specific work samples, anecdotal records of behavior, etc., that demonstrate clearly the concerns you have. Be a good listener and hear the parent's comments and explanations.

61. **A ruling pertaining to the use of evaluation procedures later consolidated in Public Law 94 – 142 resulted from which court case listed?**
(Average)

    A. Diana v. the State Board of Education (1970)

    B. Wyatt v. Stickney

    C. Larry P. v. Riles

    D. PASE v. Hannon

Answer: A. Diana v. the State Board of Education (1970)
Diana v. the State Board of Education resulted in the decision that all children must be evaluated in their native language.

62. **Included in data brought to the attention of Congress regarding the evaluation procedures for education of students with disabilities was the fact that:**
(Easy)

    A. There were a large number of children and youths with disabilities in the United States.

    B. Many children with disabilities were not receiving an appropriate education.

    C. Many parents of children with disabilities were forced to seek services outside of the public realm.

    D. All of the above

Answer: D. All of the above
All three factors, and many more, have driven Congress to act.

63. **The Individuals with Disabilities Education Act (IDEA) was signed into law in and later reauthorized through a second revision in what years?**
(Rigorous)

   A.   1975 and 2004

   B.   1980 and 1990

   C.   1990 and 2004

   D.   1995 and 2001

Answer: C. 1990 and 2004
IDEA, Public Law 101-476, is a consolidation and reauthorization of all prior special education mandates, with amendments. It was signed into law by President Bush on October 30, 1990. Revision of IDEA occurred in 2004, and IDEA was re-authorized as the Individuals with Disabilities Education Improvement Act of 2004 (IDEIA 2004). IDEIA 2004 is commonly referred to as IDEA 2004 and was effective on July 1, 2005.

64. **How was the training of special education teachers changed by the No Child Left Behind Act of 2002?**
(Rigorous)

   A.   It required all special education teachers to be certified in reading and math.

   B.   It required all special education teachers to take the same coursework as general education teachers.

   C.   If a special education teacher is teaching a core subject, he or she must meet the standard of a highly-qualified teacher in that subject.

   D.   All of the above

Answer: C. If a special education teacher is teaching a core subject, he or she must meet the standard of a highly-qualified teacher in that subject.
In order for special education teachers to be a student's sole teacher of a core subject, they must meet the professional criteria of NCLB. They must be *highly qualified*, that is certified or licensed in their area of special education, and show proof of a specific level of professional development in the core subjects that they teach. As special education teachers receive specific education in the core subject they teach, they will be better prepared to teach to the same level of learning standards as the general education teacher.

65. **The No Child Left Behind Act (NCLB) affected students with Limited English Proficiency (LEP) by:**
(Rigorous)

   A. Requiring these students to demonstrate English Language Proficiency before a High School Diploma is granted.

   B. Providing allowances for schools not to require them to take and pass state Reading Exams (RCTs) if the students were enrolled in U.S. schools for less than a year.

   C. Providing allowances for these students to opt out of state math tests if the students were enrolled in a U.S. school for less than one year.

   D. Both B and C

Answer: A. Requiring these students to demonstrate English Language Proficiency before a High School Diploma is granted.
The No Child Left Behind Act (NCLB) requires these students to demonstrate English Language Proficiency before a High School Diploma is granted.

66. **Which of the following is a specific change of language in the IDEA?**
(Rigorous)

   A. The term "Disorder" changed to "Disability."

   B. The term "Children" changed to "Children and Youth."

   C. The term "Handicapped" changed to "Impairments."

   D. The term "Handicapped" changed to "With Disabilities."

Answer: D. The term "Handicapped" changed to "With Disabilities."
"Children" became "individuals," highlighting the fact that some students with special needs were adolescents, not just "children". The word "handicapped" was changed to "with disabilities," denoting the difference between limitations imposed by society (handicap) and an inability to do certain things (disability). "With disabilities" also demonstrates that the person is thought of first, and the disabling condition is but one of the characteristics of the individual.

67. **Which component changed with the reauthorization of the Education for all Handicapped Children Act of 1975 (EHA) 1990 EHA Amendment?**
    (Rigorous)

    A.   Specific terminology

    B.   Due process protections

    C.   Non-discriminatory reevaluation procedures

    D.   Individual education plans

Answer: A. Specific terminology.

68. **Donna has been labeled "learning disabled" since second grade and has developed a fear of not being able to keep up with her peers. She has just entered middle school with a poor self-concept and often acts out to cover up her fear of failure. What is the most appropriate action her teacher can take when Donna exhibits minor inappropriate behavior?**
    (Rigorous)

    A.   Ignore the behavior unless it is too dangerous or distracting.

    B.   Praise her for her correct behavior and responses.

    C.   Discuss the inappropriate behavior tactfully and in private.

    D.   All of the above.

Answer: D. All of the above
All three of the actions listed will help correct the minor inappropriate behavior, while at the same time helping to improve the child's self-concept.

69. **Which of the following is the first step you should take to prepare to teach preparation for social situations?**
    (Average)

    A. Allow students to plan events.

    B. Lecture.

    C. Anticipate possible problems.

    D. Take your students to the anticipated setting.

Answer: C. Anticipate possible problems.
Look at all the things that could go wrong first. Chances are that if you are not prepared, an embarrassing situation could occur.

70. **The opportunity for persons with disabilities to live as close to a normal life as possible describes:**
    (Average)

    A. Least restrictive environment

    B. Normalization

    C. Mainstreaming

    D. Deinstitutionalization

Answer: B. Normalization
The other terms listed all refer to specific types of opportunities for normalization for persons with disabilities.

71. Requirements for evaluations were changed in IDEA 2004 to reflect that no 'single' assessment or measurement tool can be used to determine special education qualification, furthering that there was a disproportionate representation of what types of students? *(Average)*

    A.   Disabled

    B.   Foreign

    C.   Gifted

    D.   Minority and bilingual

Answer: D. Minority and bilingual
IDEA 2004 recognized that there exists a disproportionate representation of minorities and bilingual students and that pre-service interventions that are *scientifically based on early reading programs, positive behavioral interventions and support,* and early intervening services may prevent some of those children from needing special education services. In addition, it recognized that students whose native language is not English do not have a language disability. They simply need to learn English.

72. **What determines whether a person is entitled to protection under Section 504?**
    (Average)

    A. The individual must meet the definition of a person with a disability.

    B. The person must be able to meet the requirements of a particular program in spite of his or her disability.

    C. The school, business, or other facility must be the recipient of federal funding assistance.

    D. All of the above

Answer: D. All of the above
To be entitled to protection under Section 504, an individual must meet the definition of a person with a disability, which is: any person who (i) has a physical or mental impairment which substantially limits one or more of that person's major life activities, (ii) has a record of such impairment, or (iii) is regarded as having such an impairment. Major life activities are: caring for oneself, performing manual tasks, walking, seeing, hearing, speaking, breathing, learning, and working. The person must also be "otherwise qualified," which means that the person must be able to meet the requirements of a particular program in spite of the disability. The person must also be afforded "reasonable accommodations" by recipients of federal financial assistance.

73. Legislation in Public Law 94 – 142 attempts to:
(Rigorous)

- A. Match the child's educational needs with appropriate educational services.

- B. Include parents in the decisions made about their child's education.

- C. Establish a means by which parents can provide input.

- D. All of the above

Answer: D All of the above

Much of what was stated in separate court rulings and mandated legislation was brought together into what is now considered to be the "backbone" of special education. Public Law 94 – 142 (Education for All Handicapped Children Act) was signed into law by President Ford in 1975. It was the culmination of a great deal of litigation and legislation from the late 1960's to the mid 1970's that included decisions supporting the need to assure an appropriate education to all persons regardless of race, creed, or disability. In 1990, this law was reauthorized and renamed the Individuals with Disabilities Education Act, IDEA.

74. Effective transition was included in:
(Rigorous)

- A. President Bush's 1990 State of the Union Message

- B. Public Law 101-476

- C. Public Law 95-207

- D. Both A and B

Answer: D. Both A and B

With the enactment of P. L. 101-476 (IDEA), transition services became a right.

75. The Free and Appropriate Public Education (FAPE) describes Special Education and related services as?
(Easy)

- A. Public expenditure and standard to the state educational agency.

- B. Provided in conformity with each student's individualized education program, if the program is developed to meet requirements of the law.

- C. Including preschool, elementary, and/or secondary education in the state involved.

- D. All of the above

Answer: D. All of the above
FAPE states that special education and related services are provided at public expense; meet the standards of the state educational agency; include preschool, elementary, and/or secondary education in the state involved; and are provided in conformity with each student's IEP if the program is developed to meet requirements of the law.

76. Jane is a third grader. Mrs. Smith, her teacher, noted that Jane was having difficulty with math and reading assignments. The results from recent diagnostic tests showed a strong sight vocabulary and strength in computational skills, but a weakness in comprehending what she read. This weakness was apparent in mathematical word problems as well. The multi-disciplinary team recommended placement in a special education resource room for learning disabilities two periods each school day. For the remainder of the school day, her placement will be:
(Easy)

   A.   In the regular classroom

   B.   At a special school

   C.   In a self-contained classroom

   D.   In a resource room for intellectual disabilities

Answer: A. In the regular classroom
The resource room is a special room inside the school environment where the child goes to be taught by a teacher who is certified in the area of disability. We hope the accommodations and services provided in the resource room will help her to catch up and perform with her peers in the regular classroom.

77. **Which of the following must be provided in a written notice to parents when proposing a child's educational placement?**
    (Average)

    A. A list of parental due process safeguards

    B. A list of current test scores

    C. A list of persons responsible for the child's education

    D. A list of academic subjects the child has passed

Answer: A. A list of parental due process safeguards
Written notice must be provided to parents prior to a proposal or refusal to initiate or make a change in the child's identification, evaluation, or educational placement. Notices must contain:
- A listing of parental due process safeguards
- A description and a rationale for the chosen action
- A detailed listing of components (e.g., tests, records, reports) that were the basis for the decision
- Assurance that the language and content of the notices were understood by the parents

78. **Zero Reject requires all children with disabilities be provided with what?**
    (Average)

    A. Total exclusion of functional exclusion

    B. Adherence to the annual local education agency (LEA) reporting

    C. Free, appropriate public education

    D. Both B and C

Answer: C. Free, appropriate public education
The principle of zero reject requires that all children with disabilities be provided with a free, appropriate public education, and the LEA reporting procedure locates, identifies, and evaluates children with disabilities within a given jurisdiction to ensure their attendance in public school.

79. **Students who receive special services in a regular classroom with consultation generally have academic and/or social-interpersonal performance deficits at which level of severity?**
    (Easy)

    A.   Mild

    B.   Moderate

    C.   Severe

    D.   Profound

Answer: A. Mild
The majority of students receiving special services are enrolled primarily in regular classes. Those with mild learning and behavior problems exhibit academic and/or social interpersonal deficits that are often evident only in a school-related setting. These students appear no different to their peers, physically.

80. **The greatest number of students receiving special services is enrolled primarily in:**
    (Average)

    A.   The regular classroom

    B.   The resource room

    C.   Self-contained classrooms

    D.   Special schools

Answer: A. The regular classroom
See previous question.

81. **The most restrictive environment in which an individual might be placed and receive instruction is that of:**
    (Easy)

    A. Institutional setting

    B. Homebound instruction

    C. Special schools

    D. Self-contained special classes

Answer: A. Institutional setting
Individuals who require significantly modified environments for care treatment and accommodation are usually educated in an institutional setting. They usually have profound/multiple disorders.

82. **The law affects required components of the IEP; elements required by the IEP and the law are:**
    (Rigorous)

    A. Present level of academic and functional performance; statement of how the disability affects the student's involvement and progress; evaluation criteria and timeliness for instructional objective achievement; modifications of accommodations

    B. Projected dates for services initiation with anticipated frequency, location and duration; statement of when parent will be notified; statement of annual goals

    C. Extent to which child will not participate in regular education program; transitional needs for students age 14.

    D. All of the above.

Answer: D. All of the above
IEPs outline very specific elements that are required, and you may review them in Skill 1.3 under IEP. Educators must keep themselves apprised of the changes and amendments to laws, such as IDEA 2004, with addendums released in October of 2006.

83. **IEPs continue to have multiple sections; one section, present levels, now addresses what?**
    (Average)

    A. Academic achievement and functional performance

    B. English as a second language

    C. Functional performance

    D. Academic achievement

Answer: A. Academic achievement and functional performance
Individualized Education Plans (IEPS) continue to have multiple sections. One section, present levels, now addresses academic achievement and functional performance. Annual IEP goals must now address the same areas.

84. **What is true about IDEA? In order to be eligible, a student must:**
    (Easy)

    A. Have a medical disability

    B. Have a disability that fits into one of the categories listed in the law

    C. Attend a private school

    D. Be a slow learner

Answer: B. Have a disability that fits into one of the categories listed in the law
IDEA is a legal instrument; thus, it is defined by law. Every aspect in the operation of IDEA is laid out in law.

85. Changes in requirements for Current Levels of performance require: *(Average)*

    A. student voice in each Present Level of Performance.

    B. CSE chair must tell parents when child has unrealistic goals.

    C. Parent/Guardian must attend either by phone conference or in person.

    D. Teachers must write post adult outcomes assigning a student to a specific field.

Answer: A. student voice in each Present Level of Performance
Idea's new Indicator 13 is changing the way IEPs are written. The federal government is requiring changes in IEPs to create an easier way to collect statistics on student success at reaching post school goals. While many of the requirements have been used for years, compliance is now being measured by the items listed below.

Present Levels of Performance: Student voice must be included in each Present Level of Performance. This means that Academic, Social, Physical, Management, etc. must include one student voice statement either in the strengths or needs or both. For example, "John reads fluently on a 3rd grade level. He is able to add and subtract two digit numbers. He has difficulty with grouping and multiplying. *John states that he would rather read than do math.*" Student voice can express either his/her strengths, preferences and/or interests. When the child begins to do vocational assessments, student voice should be related to transition to post-school activities of his/her choice. In addition, Present Levels of Performance must indicate why a student's post adult goals are realistic, or why they are not.

86. **Developmental Disabilities:**
    (Rigorous)

    A. Is the categorical name for intellectual disabilities in IDEA

    B. Includes congenital conditions, such as severe Spina Bifida, deafness, blindness, or profound intellectual disabilities

    C. Includes children who contract diseases, such as polio or meningitis, and who are left in an incapacitated functional state

    D. Both B and C

Answer: D. Both B and C
Developmental disabilities include congenital conditions and children who contract diseases and are left in an incapacitated functional state.

87. **Which of the following goals reflects new IDEA requirements?**
    (Rigorous)

    A. Janet wants to be a doctor.

    B. Frank intends to go to The Culinary Institute.

    C. Janet will go to college.

    D. Carmel currently lives independently on her own.

Answer: C. Janet will go to college.
Post adult outcome must now be written with a "student will" statement.

88. **The definition for "Other Health Impaired (OHI)" in IDEA:**
(Rigorous)

    A. Is the definition that accepts heart conditions

    B. Includes deafness, blindness, or profound intellectual disabilities

    C. Includes Autism and PDD

    D. Includes cochlear implants

Answer: A. Is the definition that accepts heart conditions
This is the definition that accepts heart conditions. OHI includes a variety of reasons and diagnoses, including heart conditions.

89. **Which is an educational characteristic common to students with mild intellectual learning and behavioral disabilities?**
(Easy)

    A. Show interest in schoolwork

    B. Have intact listening skills

    C. Require modification in classroom instruction

    D. Respond better to passive than to active learning tasks

Answer: C. Require modification in classroom instruction
Some of the characteristics of students with mild learning and behavioral disabilities are as follows: Lack of interest in schoolwork; prefer concrete rather than abstract lessons; weak listening skills; low achievement; limited verbal and/or writing skills; respond better to active rather than passive learning tasks; have areas of talent or ability often overlooked by teachers; prefer to receive special help in regular classroom; higher dropout rate than regular education students; achieve in accordance with teacher expectations; require modification in classroom instruction; and are easily distracted.

90. In general, characteristics of students with learning disabilities include:
(Average)

    A.   A low level of performance in a majority of academic skill areas

    B.   Limited cognitive ability

    C.   A discrepancy between achievement and potential

    D.   A uniform pattern of academic development

Answer: C A discrepancy between achievement and potential
The individual with a specific learning disability exhibits a discrepancy between achievement and potential.

91. Michael's teacher complains that he is constantly out of his seat. She also reports that he has trouble paying attention to what is going on in class for more than a couple of minutes at a time. He appears to be trying, but his writing is often illegible, containing many reversals. Although he seems to want to please, he is very impulsive and stays in trouble with his teacher. He is failing reading, and his math grades, though somewhat better, are still below average. Michael's psychometric evaluation should include assessment for:
(Average)

   A. Mild intellectual disabilities

   B. Specific learning disabilities

   C. Mild behavior disorders

   D. Hearing impairment

Answer: B Specific learning disabilities
Some of the characteristics of persons with learning disabilities are:
- Hyperactivity: a rate of motor activity higher than normal
- Perceptual difficulties: visual, auditory, and haptic perceptual problems
- Perceptual-motor impairments: poor integration of visual and motor systems, often affecting fine motor coordination
- Disorders of memory and thinking: memory deficits, trouble with problem-solving, concept formation and association, poor awareness of own metacognitive skills (learning strategies)
- Impulsiveness: acts before considering consequences, poor impulse control, often followed by remorselessness
- Academic problems in reading, math, writing or spelling; significant discrepancies in ability levels

92. Joey is in a mainstreamed preschool program. One of the means his teacher uses in determining growth in adaptive skills is that of observation. Some questions about Joey's behavior that she might ask include:
    (Average)

    A. Is he able to hold a cup?

    B. Can he call the name of any of his toys?

    C. Can he reach for an object and grasp it?

    D. All of the above

Answer: D. All of the above
Here are some characteristics of individuals with intellectual disabilities or intellectual
disabilities:
- IQ of 70 or below
- Limited cognitive ability; delayed academic achievement, particularly in language-related subjects
- Deficits in memory, which often relate to poor initial perception, or inability to apply stored information to relevant situations
- Impaired formulation of learning strategies
- Difficulty in attending to relevant aspects of stimuli: slowness in reaction time or in employing alternate strategies
- Deficits in many adaptive behavior skills

93. Individuals with intellectual disabilities can be characterized as:
    (Rigorous)

    A. Often indistinguishable from normal developing children at an early age

    B. Having a higher than normal rate of motor activity

    C. Displaying significant discrepancies in ability levels

    D. Uneducable in academic skills

Answer: A. Often indistinguishable from normal developing children at an early age
See rationale for question 32 for some characteristics of individuals with intellectual disabilities or intellectual disabilities.

94. **Which of the following statements about children with an emotional/behavioral disorder is true?**
   (Average)

   A. They have very high IQs.

   B. They display poor social skills.

   C. They are poor academic achievers.

   D. Both B and C

Answer: D. Both B and C
Children who exhibit mild behavioral disorders are characterized by:
- Average or above average scores on intelligence tests
- Poor academic achievement; learned helplessness
- Unsatisfactory interpersonal relationships
- Immaturity; attention seeking
- Aggressive, acting-out behavior: (hitting, fighting, teasing, yelling, refusing to comply with requests, excessive attention seeking, poor anger control, temper tantrums, hostile reactions, defiant use of language) OR Anxious, withdrawn behavior: (infantile behavior, social isolation, few friends, withdrawal into fantasy, fears, hypochondria, unhappiness, crying)

95. **Which behavior would be expected at the mild level of emotional/behavioral disorders?**
   (Average)

   A. Attention seeking

   B. Inappropriate affect

   C. Self-Injurious

   D. Poor sense of identity

Answer: A. Attention seeking
See rationale to question 34.

96. **Children with disabilities are LEAST likely to improve their social-interpersonal skills by:**
    (Rigorous)

    A. Developing sensitivity to other people

    B. Making behavioral choices in social situations

    C. Developing social maturity

    D. Talking with their sister or brother

Answer: D. Talking with their sister or brother
The social skills of the child are known in the family and seen as "normal" for him/her. Regular conversation with a family member would be the least conducive to improving social skills. Remember, the purpose in building social-interpersonal skills is to improve a person's ability to maintain interdependent relationships between persons.

97. **Autism is a condition characterized by:**
    (Easy)

    A. Distorted relationships with others

    B. Perceptual anomalies

    C. Self-stimulation

    D. All of the above

Answer: D. All of the above
See previous question.

98. **As a separate exceptionality category in IDEA, autism:**
    (Average)

    A. Includes emotional/behavioral disorders as defined in federal regulations

    B. Adversely affects educational performance

    C. Is thought to be a form of mental illness

    D. Is a developmental disability that affects verbal and non-verbal communication

Answer: D. Is a developmental disability that affects verbal and non-verbal communication
See rationale to question 36.

99. **Normality in child behavior is influenced by society's:**
    (Average)

    A. Attitudes and cultural beliefs

    B. Hereditary factors

    C. Prenatal care

    D. Attitudes and Victorian era motto

Answer: A. Attitudes and cultural beliefs
Society's attitudes and cultural beliefs influence normality and the perception of normality in child behavior.

100. The CST coordinates and participates in due diligence through what process?
(Average)

- A. Child study team meets for the first time without parents.

- B. Teachers take child learning concerns to the school counselor.

- C. School counselor contacts parents for permission to perform screening assessments.

- D. All of the above

Answer: D. All of the above
The CST coordinates and participates in due diligence through a process that includes teachers' or parents' concerns about academic or functional development and goes to the counselor who then obtains permission for screening assessments of child's skills, and the results determine need. If needed, the child study team meets without parents first.

101. Which of the following examples would be considered of highest priority when determining the need for the delivery of appropriate special education and related services?
    (Rigorous)

    A. An eight-year-old boy is repeating first grade for the second time and exhibits problems with toileting, gross motor functions, and remembering number and letter symbols. His regular classroom teacher claims the referral forms are too time-consuming and refuses to complete them. He also refuses to make accommodations because he feels every child should be treated alike.

    B. A six-year-old girl who has been diagnosed as autistic is placed in a special education class within the local school. Her mother wants her to attend residential school next year even though the girl is showing progress.

    C. A ten-year-old girl with profound intellectual disabilities who is receiving education services in a state institution.

    D. A twelve-year-old boy with mild disabilities who was placed in a behavior disorders program but displays obvious perceptual deficits (e.g., reversal of letters and symbols and inability to discriminate sounds). He originally was thought to have a learning disability but did not meet state criteria for this exceptionality category based on results of standard scores. He has always had problems with attending to a task and is now beginning to get into trouble during seatwork time. His teacher feels that he will eventually become a real behavior problem. He receives social skills training in the resource room one period a day.

Answer: A. An eight-year-old boy is repeating first grade for the second time and exhibits problems with toileting, gross motor functions, and remembering number and letter symbols. His regular classroom teacher claims the referral forms are too time-consuming and refuses to complete them. He also refuses to make accommodations because he feels every child should be treated alike.

No modifications are being made, so the child is not receiving any services whatsoever. Note also, that the teacher in this scenario is in violation of the law.

102. When a student is identified as being at-risk academically or socially what does Federal law hope for first?
(Rigorous)

	A.	Move the child quickly to assessment.

	B.	Place the child in special education as soon as possible.

	C.	Observe the child to determine what is wrong.

	D.	Perform remedial intervention in the classroom.

Answer: D. Perform remedial intervention in the classroom.
Once a student is identified as being at-risk academically or socially, remedial interventions are attempted within the regular classroom. Federal legislation requires that sincere efforts be made to help the child learn in the regular classroom.

103. What do the 9th and 10th Amendments to the U.S. Constitution state about education?
(Average)

	A.	That education belongs to the people

	B.	That education is an unstated power vested in the states

	C.	That elected officials mandate education

	D.	That education is free

Answer: B. That education is an unstated power vested in the states
The 9th and 10th Amendments state that education is an unstated power vested in the states.

104. The IDEA states that child assessment is?
(Average)

- A. At intervals with teacher discretion
- B. Continuous on a regular basis
- C. Left to the counselor
- D. Conducted annually

Answer: B. Continuous on a regular basis
Assessments in Special Education are continuous and occur on a regular basis.

105. Safeguards against bias and discrimination in the assessment of children include:
(Average)

- A. The testing of a child in Standard English
- B. The requirement for the use of one standardized test
- C. The use of evaluative materials in the child's native language or other mode of communication
- D. All testing performed by a certified, licensed psychologist

Answer: C. The use of evaluative materials in the child's native language or other mode of communication
The law requires that the child be evaluated in his native language or mode of communication. The idea that a licensed psychologist evaluates the child does not meet the criteria if it is not done in the child's normal mode of communication.

106. Which is characteristic of group tests?
(Average)

   A. Directions are always read to students.

   B. The examiner monitors several students at the same time.

   C. The teacher must follow a standardized procedure.

   D. Diagnostic information cannot be gathered.

Answer: B. The examiner monitors several students at the same time.
The group test variable simply refers to the manner of presentation of the test. A group test is given to more than one student at a time and the teacher monitors all the students taking the test simultaneously. Group assessments can be formal or informal, standardized or not, criterion or norm referenced. Individual assessments can be found in all these types, as well.

107. For which of the following uses are standardized individual tests MOST appropriate?
(Rigorous)

   A. Screening students to determine possible need for special education services

   B. Evaluation of special education curricula

   C. Tracking of gifted students

   D. Evaluation of a student for eligibility and placement, or individualized program planning, in special education

Answer: D. Evaluation of a student for eligibility and placement, or individualized program planning, in special education
See previous question. Standardized tests are useful for these decisions, because they are very objective and can provide a wide range of data, from comparison with grade peers (a norm-referenced test), to mastery of certain skills (criterion referenced test), to pinpointing specific areas of strength or weakness (intelligence tests or psychological tests).

108. Which of the following is an advantage of giving informal, individual rather than standardized group tests?
(Easy)

    A.   Questions can be modified to reveal a specific student's strategies or misconceptions..

    B.   The test administrator can clarify or rephrase questions.

    C.   They can be inserted into the class quickly on an as needed basis.

    D.   All of the above

Answer: D. All of the above

Standardized group tests are administered to a group in a specifically prescribed manner, with strict rules to keep procedures, scoring, and interpretation of results uniform in all cases. Such tests allow comparisons to be made across populations, ages or grades. *Informal* assessments have less objective measures, and may include anecdotes or observations that may or may not be quantified, interviews, informal questioning during a task, etc. An example of an informal *individually* administered assessment might be watching a student sort objects to see what attribute is most important to the student, or questioning a student to see what he or she found confusing about a task. All of the answers listed are advantages of giving informal individual rather than standardized group tests. Since standardized tests require rigid adherence to a precise format and presentation, they do not have the flexibility needed to modify questions to follow an individual student's strategies or needs as they work.

109. Mrs. Stokes has been teaching her third grade students about mammals during a recent science unit. Which of the following would be true of a criterion-referenced test she might administer at the conclusion of the unit?
(Average)

   A.   It will be based on unit objectives.

   B.   Derived scores will be used to rank student achievement.

   C.   Standardized scores are effective of national performance samples.

   D.   All of the above

Answer: A. It will be based on unit objectives.
Criterion-referenced tests measure the progress made by individuals in mastering specific skills. The content is based on a specific set of objectives rather than on the general curriculum. Criterion-referenced tests provide measurements pertaining to the information a given student needs to know and the skills that student needs to master.

110. For which of the following purposes is a norm-referenced test LEAST appropriate?
(Rigorous)

   A.   Screening

   B.   Individual program planning

   C.   Program evaluation

   D.   Making placement decisions

Answer: B. Individual program planning
Norm-referenced tests provide a means of comparing a student's performance to the performance typically expected of others the same age or grade but should not be used for individual program planning. Norm-referenced tests have a large advantage over criterion-referenced tests when used for screening or program evaluation. Norm-referenced tests provide a means of comparing a student's performance to the performance typically expected of others of his age or grade

111. Criterion-referenced tests can provide information about:
(Rigorous)

- A. Whether a student has mastered prerequisite skills

- B. Whether a student is ready to proceed to the next level of instruction

- C. Which instructional materials might be helpful in covering program objectives

- D. All of the above

Answer: A. Whether a student has mastered prerequisite skills
In criterion-referenced testing, the emphasis is on assessing specific and relevant behaviors that have been mastered. Items on criterion-referenced tests are often linked directly to specific instructional objectives.

112. Which of the following purposes of testing calls for an informal test?
(Average)

- A. Screening a group of children to determine their readiness for the first reader.

- B. Analyzing the responses of a student with a disability to various presentations of content material to see which strategy works for him.

- C. Evaluating the effectiveness of a fourth grade math program at the end of its first year of use in a specific school..

- D. Determining the general level of intellectual functioning of a class of fifth graders.

Answer: B. Analyzing the responses of a student with a disability to various presentations of content material to see which strategy works for him.
Formal tests, such as standardized tests or textbook quizzes are objective tests that include primarily questions for which there is only one correct answer. Some are teacher prepared, but many are commercially prepared and frequently standardized. To analyze the response of a student to different types of instructional presentation informal methods such as observation and questioning are more useful.

113. Which of the following is not a true statement about informal tests? *(Average)*

A. Informal tests are useful in comparing students to others of their age or grade level.

B. The correlation between curriculum and test criteria is much higher in informal tests.

C. Informal tests are useful in evaluating n individual's response to instruction.

D. Informal tests are used to diagnose a student's particular strengths and weaknesses for purpose of planning individual programs.

Answer: A. Informal tests are useful in comparing students to others of their age or grade..

Informal tests do NOT allow comparison among students of the same age or grade. Norm referenced tests are standardized tests that compare a student's responses to those of a large population of the same age or grade. Informal tests are not useful in comparing students to others in the population because they are neither standardized nor normed. Informal tests are often teacher made and usually criterion referenced. They are useful for a variety of diagnostic and instructional planning purposes.

114. For which situation might a teacher be apt to select a formal test? *(Rigorous)*

A. A pretest for studying world religions

B. A weekly spelling test

C. To compare student progress with that of peers of same age or grade level on a national basis

D. To determine which content objectives outlined on the student's IEP were mastered

Answer: C. To compare student progress with that of peers of same age or grade level on a national basis

See previous question.

115. The Key Math Diagnostic Arithmetic Test is an individually administered test of math skills. It is comprised of fourteen subtests, which are classified into the major math areas of content, operations, and applications for which subtest scores are reported. The test manual describes the population sample upon which the test was normed and reports data pertaining to reliability and validity. In addition, for each item in the test, a behavioral objective is presented. From the description, it can be determined that this achievement test is:
(Rigorous)

- A. Individually administered
- B. Criterion-referenced
- C. Diagnostic
- D. All of the above

Answer: D. All of the above
The test has a limited content designed to measure to what extent the student has mastered specific areas in math. The expressions "individually administered" and "diagnostic" appear in the description of the test.

116. The best measures of a student's functional capabilities and entry-level skills are:
(Rigorous)

- A. Norm-referenced tests
- B. Teacher-made post-tests
- C. Standardized IQ tests
- D. Criterion-referenced measures

Answer: D. Criterion-referenced measures
Criterion-referenced measures are useful for assessment of a student's functional capabilities and entry-level skills. Unlike norm-referenced tests, which compare an individual with others of the same grade or age level, criterion-referenced tests, measure the level of functions and skills of the individual.

117. One of your students receives a percentile rank of 45 on a standardized test. This indicates that the student's score:
(Rigorous)

- A. Consisted of 45 correct answers
- B. Was at the point above which 45% of the other scores fell
- C. Was at the point below which 45% of the other scores fell
- D. Was below passing

Answer: C. Was at the point below which 45% of the other scores fell
Percentile scores indicate how well the student did compared to the other students tested. A percentile rank of 45 indicates that the student's score was at the point below which 45% of the other scores fell.

118. When you need to evaluate a student's work ethics, you should give what assessment?
(Rigorous)

- A. Naturalistic
- B. Dynamic
- C. Performance-based
- D. Criterion-referenced

Answer: A. Naturalistic
Work ethics are social skills. Social skills are best evaluated over time in their natural surroundings.

119. Alternative assessments include all of the following EXCEPT:
(Average)

- A. Portfolios

- B. Interviews

- C. Textbook chapter tests

- D. Student choice of assessment format

Answer: C. Textbook chapter tests
Textbook chapter tests are formal, usually multiple choice tests with one fixed, correct answer. Portfolios, interviews and student choices in assessment format are alternative assessments with flexible formats and alternative, individually based, criteria.

120. Which of the following is an example of an alternative assessment?
(Rigorous)

- A. Testing skills in a "real world" setting in several settings

- B. Pre-test of student knowledge of fractions before beginning wood shop

- C. Answering an essay question that allows for creative thought

- D. A compilation of a series of tests in a portfolio

Answer: A. Testing skills in a "real world" setting in several settings
Naturalistic assessment is a form of alternative assessment that requires testing in actual application settings of life skills. The skill of using money correctly could be correctly assessed in this method by taking the student shopping in different settings.

PRE-TEST ANSWER KEY

1.	A		31.	B
2.	B		32.	B
3.	D		33.	A
4.	C		34.	D
5.	A		35.	D
6.	C		36.	B
7.	C		37.	A
8.	C		38.	D
9.	C		39.	C
10.	B		40.	D
11.	C		41.	D
12.	C		42.	C
13.	D		43.	D
14.	D		44.	C
15.	C		45.	B
16.	A		46.	A
17.	A		47.	B
18.	D		48.	A
19.	C		49.	C
20.	C		50.	A
21.	A		51.	C
22.	D		52.	D
23.	A		53.	D
24.	B		54.	C
25.	B		55.	D
26.	A		56.	C
27.	B		57.	C
28.	A		58.	C
29.	B		59.	A
30.	C		60.	C

61.	A	91.	B
62.	D	92.	D
63.	C	93.	A
64.	C	94.	D
65.	A	95.	A
66.	D	96.	D
67.	A	97.	D
68.	D	98.	D
69.	C	99.	A
70.	B	100.	D
71.	D	101.	A
72.	D	102.	D
73.	D	103.	B
74.	D	104.	B
75.	D	105.	C
76.	A	106.	B
77.	A	107.	D
78.	C	108.	D
79.	A	109.	A
80.	A	110.	B
81.	A	111.	A
82.	D	112.	B
83.	A	113.	A
84.	B	114.	C
85.	A	115.	D
86.	D	116.	D
87.	C	117.	C
88.	A	118.	A
89.	C	119.	C
90.	C	120.	A

PRE-TEST RIGOR TABLE

	Easy 19%	Average 40%	Rigorous 41%
Question	10, 14, 25, 32, 34, 37, 41, 43, 44, 48, 50, 53, 54, 60, 61, 75, 76, 79, 81, 84, 89, 97, 108	1, 3, 5, 12, 16, 18, 19, 20, 29, 30, 33, 35, 39, 45, 49, 51, 52, 55, 56, 57, 58, 59, 61, 69, 70, 71, 72, 77, 78, 80, 83, 85, 90, 91, 92, 94, 95, 98, 99, 100, 103, 104, 105, 106, 109, 112, 113, 119	2, 4, 6, 7, 8, 9, 11, 13, 15, 17, 21, 22, 23, 24, 26, 27, 28, 31, 36, 38, 40, 42, 46, 47, 63, 64, 65, 66, 67, 68, 73, 74, 82, 86, 87, 88, 93, 96, 101, 102, 107, 110, 111, 114, 115, 116, 117, 118, 120

PRAXIS Special Education Practice Test Kit
Post-Test Sample Questions

1. Howard has been diagnosed as having maladaptive behavior of an immature/anxious withdrawn nature. A behavior that we might expect of Howard, considering his diagnosis is:
   (Rigorous)

   A. Resistance

   B. Teasing

   C. Fantasizing

   D. Hostility

2. Which of these is listed as only a minor scale on the Behavior Problem Checklist?
   (Average)

   A. Motor Excess

   B. Conduct Disorder

   C. Socialized Aggression

   D. Anxiety/Withdrawal

3. Kenny, a fourth grader, has trouble comprehending analogies, using comparative, spatial, and temporal words, and multiple meanings. Language interventions for Kenny would focus on:
   (Rigorous)

   A. Morphology

   B. Syntax

   C. Pragmatics

   D. Semantics

4. Five-year-old Tom continues to substitute the "w" sound for the "r" sound when pronouncing words; therefore, he often distorts words e.g., "wabbit" for "rabbit" and "wat" for "rat." His articulation disorder is basically a problem in:
   (Rigorous)

   A. Phonology

   B. Morphology

   C. Syntax

   D. Semantics

5. **The Carrow Elicited Language Inventory is a test designed to give the examiner diagnostic information about a child's expressive grammatical competence. Which of the following language components is being assessed?**
(Rigorous)

   A. Phonology

   B. Morphology

   C. Syntax

   D. Both B and C

6. **At what stage of cognitive development might we expect a student to being to think about and systematically consider possible future goals?**
(Average)

   A. Early Adolescence

   B. Middle Adolescence

   C. Late Adolescence

   D. Adulthood

7. **Which of the following manifestations can be characteristic of students placed in the exceptionality category of Other Health Impaired?**
(Average)

   A. Limited strength, vitality, or alertness

   B. Severe communication and developmental problems

   C. Chronic or acute health problems

   D. All of the above

8. **A developmental delay may be indicated by a:**
(Rigorous)

   A Second grader having difficulty buttoning clothing

   B. Stuttered response

   C. Kindergartner not having complete bladder control

   D. Withdrawn behavior

9. **Which is *least* indicative of a developmental delay?**
(Rigorous)

   A. Deficits in language and speech production

   B. Deficits in gross motor skills

   C. Deficits in self-help skills

   D. Deficits in arithmetic computation skills

10. **An organic reason for mild learning and behavioral disabilities is:**
    (Rigorous)

    A. Inadequate education

    B. Toxins

    C. Biochemical factors

    D. Nutrition

11. **Of the various factors that contribute to delinquency and anti-social behavior, which has been found to be the weakest?**
    (Rigorous)

    A. Criminal behavior and/or alcoholism in the father

    B. Lax mother and punishing father

    C. Socioeconomic disadvantage

    D. Long history of broken home and marital discord among parents

12. **Criteria for choosing behaviors to measure by frequency include all but those that:**
    (Easy)

    A. Have an observable beginning

    B. Last a long time

    C. Last a short time

    D. Occur often

13. **Ryan is three and her temper tantrums last for an hour. Bryan is eight and he does not stay on task for more than ten minutes without teacher prompts. These behaviors differ from normal children in terms of their:**
    (Average)

    A. Rate

    B. Topography

    C. Duration

    D. Magnitude

14. **The most direct method of obtaining assessment data, and perhaps the most objective, is:**
    (Easy)

    A. Testing

    B. Self-recording

    C. Observation

    D. Experimenting

15. **The most important member of the transition team is the:**
    (Easy)

    A. Parent

    B. Student

    C. Secondary personnel

    D. Postsecondary personnel

16. **Echolalia is a characteristic of which disability?**
    (Average)

    A. Autism

    B. Intellectual disabilities

    C. Social Pragmatic Disorder

    D. ADHD

17. **Satisfaction of the LRE requirement means that:**
    (Easy)

    A. The school is providing the best services it can offer there.

    B. The school is providing the best services the district has to offer.

    C. The student is being educated with the fewest special education services necessary.

    D The student is being educated in the least restrictive setting that meets his or her needs

18. **IDEA specified that students with disabilities must be placed in the Least Restrictive Environment (LRE). In the Cascade System of Special Education Services, which of the following would be considered the LRE for a student with a mild learning disability?**
    (Easy)

    A. A Co-Teach setting

    B. Paraprofessional support in the general education classroom

    C. A separate special education classroom

    D. There is not enough information to make that determination.

19. **Vocational training programs are based on all of the following ideas EXCEPT:**
    (Average)

    A. Students obtain career training from elementary through high school.

    B. Students acquire specific training in job skills prior to exiting school.

    C. Students need specific training and supervision in applying skills learned in school to requirements in job situations.

    D. Students obtain needed instruction and field-based experiences that help them to be able to work in specific occupations.

20. IDEA identifies specific disability conditions under which students may be eligible to receive special education services. Of the following, which is NOT a specific disability area identified in IDEA?
(Average)

    A. Other Health Impairment

    B. Emotional Disturbance

    C. Specific Learning Disability

    D. Attention Deficit Disorder

21. To be entitled to protection under Section 504, the individual must meet the definition of a person with a disability, which is any person who: 1. has a physical or mental impairment that substantially limits one or more of such person's major life activities, 2. has a record of such impairment, or 3. is regarded as having such impairment. Which of the following is considered a "major life activity"?
(Easy)

    A. Engaging in sports, hobbies, and recreation

    B. Caring for oneself

    C. Driving a car

    D. Having a social network

22. NCLB and IDEA 2004 changed Special Education Teacher requirements by:
(Easy)

    A. Requiring a Highly Qualified status for job placement

    B. Adding changes to the requirement for certifications

    C. Adding legislation requiring teachers to maintain knowledge of law

    D. Requiring inclusive environmental experience prior to certification

23. Hector is a 10th grader in a program for students with severe emotional disturbances. After a classmate taunted him about his mother, Hector threw a desk at the other boy and attacked him. A crisis intervention team tried to break up the fight, and one teacher hurt his knee. The other boy received a concussion. Hector now faces disciplinary measures. How long can he be suspended without the suspension constituting a "change of placement"?
(Rigorous)

    A. 5 days

    B. 10 days

    C. 10 + 30 days

    D. 60 days

24. *Irving Independent School District v Tatro, 1984*, is significant in its impact upon what component of the delivery of special education services?
(Average)

   A. Health Services

   B. FAPE

   C. Speech Therapy

   D. LRE

25. The family plays a vital role in our society by:
(Easy)

   A. Assuming a protective and nurturing function

   B. Acting as the primary unit for social control

   C. Playing a major role in the transmission of cultural values and morals

   D. All of the above

26. The first American school for students who are deaf was founded in 1817 by:
(Easy)

   A. Jean Marc Itard

   B. Thomas Hopkins Gallaudet

   C. Dorothea Dix

   D. Maria Montessori

27. The movement towards serving as many children with disabilities as possible in the regular classroom with supports and services grew out of:
(Average)

   A. The Full Service Model

   B. The Regular Education Model

   C. The Normalization movement

   D. The Mainstream Model

28. In successful inclusion:
(Easy)

   A. A variety of instructional arrangements is available

   B. School personnel shift the responsibility for learning outcomes to the student

   C. The physical facilities are used as they are

   D. Regular classroom teachers have sole responsibility for evaluating student progress

29. **Teaching children functional skills that will be useful in their home life and neighborhoods is the basis of:**
    (Rigorous)

    A. Curriculum-based instruction

    B. Community-based instruction

    C. Transition planning

    D. Functional curriculum

30. **The transition activities that have to be addressed, unless the IEP team finds it uncalled for, include all of the following EXCEPT:**
    (Rigorous)

    A. Instruction

    B. Volunteer opportunities

    C. Community experiences

    D. Development of objectives related to employment and other post-school areas

31. **Which learning theory emphasizes at least seven different ways in which a student learns?**
    (Average)

    A. Cognitive Approach

    B. Ecological Approach

    C. Multiple Intelligences

    D. Brain Based Learning

32. **According to Piaget's theory, a normally developing third grader would be at what stage of development?**
    (Average)

    A. Sensory motor

    B. Pre-Operational

    C. Concrete Operational

    D. Formal Operational

33. **The components that must be included in the written notice provided to parents prior to a proposal or refusal to initiate or make a change in the child's identification, evaluation, or educational placement are: 1. A listing of parental due process safeguards; 2. A description and a rationale for the chosen action; 3. Assurance that the language and content of the notices were understood by the parents; and 4. _____.**
(Rigorous)

    A. a detailed listing of components that were the basis for the decision

    B. a detailed listing of the Related Services provided by Special Education

    C. a list of the disability areas covered by IDEA

    D. the telephone numbers of local attorneys who specialize in education law

34. **What is MOST descriptive of vocational training in special education?**
(Easy)

    A. Trains students in intellectual disabilities solely.

    B. Segregates students with and without disabilities in vocational training programs.

    C. Only includes students capable of moderate supervision.

    D. Instruction focuses upon self-help skills, social- interpersonal skills, motor skills, rudimentary academic skills, simple occupational skills, and lifetime leisure and occupational skills

35. **A best practice for evaluating student performance and progress on IEPs is:**
(Rigorous)

    A. Formal assessment

    B. Curriculum-based assessment

    C. Criterion-based assessment

    D. Norm-referenced evaluation

36. Who is responsible for the implementation of a student's IEP?
(Easy)

    A. Related Service Providers

    B. General Education Teacher

    C. Special Education Teacher

    D. All of the Above

37. The components of effective lesson planning include: quizzes, or review of the previous lesson, step-by-step presentations with multiple examples, guided practice and feedback, and _____.
(Average)

    A. hands-on projects

    B. manipulative materials

    C. audio-visual aids

    D. independent practice

38. The minimum number of IEP meetings required per year is:
(Average)

    A. As many as necessary

    B. One

    C. Two

    D. Three

39. Which of these groups is not comprehensively covered by IDEA?
(Average)

    A. Gifted and talented

    B. Mentally retarded

    C. Specific learning disabilities

    D. Speech and language impaired

40. Which of the following is NOT an appropriate assessment modification or accommodation for a student with a learning disability?
(Average)

    A. Having the test read orally to the student

    B. Writing down the student's dictated answers

    C. Allowing the student to take the assessment home to complete

    D. Extending the time for the student to take the assessment

41. **Larry has a moderate intellectual disability. He will probably do best in a classroom that has:**
    (Average)

    A. A reduced class size

    B. A structured learning schedule

    C. Use of hands-on concrete learning materials and experiences

    D. All of the above

42. **A consultant teacher should be meeting the needs of his/her students by:**
    (Easy)

    A. Pushing in to do small group instruction with regular education students

    B. Asking the student to show his/her reasoning for failing

    C. Meeting with the teacher before class to discuss adaptations and expectations

    D. Accompanying the student to class

43. **Which assistive device can be used by those who are visually impaired to assist in their learning?**
    (Rigorous)

    A. Soniguide

    B. Personal Companion

    C. Closed Circuit Television (CCTV)

    D. ABVI

44. **Marisol has been mainstreamed into a ninth grade language arts class. Although her behavior is satisfactory, and she likes the class, Marisol's reading level is about two years below grade level. The class has been assigned to read *Great Expectations* and write a report. What intervention would be LEAST successful in helping Marisol complete this assignment?**
    (Average)

    A. Having Marisol listen to a taped recording while following the story in the regular text

    B. Giving her a modified version of the story

    C. Telling her to choose a different book that she can read

    D. Showing a film to the entire class and comparing and contrasting it with the book

45. Educators who advocate for educating all children in their neighborhood classrooms and schools, who propose the end of labeling and segregation of special needs students in special classes, and who call for the delivery of special supports and services directly in the classroom, may be said to support the:
(Rigorous)

A. Full service model

B. Regular education initiative

C. Full inclusion model

D. Mainstream model

46. The Peabody Individual Achievement Test (PIAT) is an individually administered test. It measures math, decoding, comprehension, spelling, and general information, and reports comparison scores. Data is offered on standardization, validity, reliability, and so on. This achievement test has features of a:
(Rigorous)

A. Norm-Referenced Test

B. Diagnostic Test

C. Screening Tool

D. A and C

47. Support can be given for all but which of the following facts? IQ scores:
(Rigorous)

A. Are interchangeable but not necessarily consistent between tests of intelligence

B. Can fluctuate over time periods

C. Measure innate intelligence

D. Are single elements of the total abilities attributable to an individual

48. Which of these would be the least effective measure of behavioral disorders?
(Easy)

A. Projective test

B. Ecological assessment

C. Achievement test

D. Psychodynamic analysis

49. Anecdotal Records should:
(Average)

A. Record observable behavior

B. End with conjecture

C. Record motivational factors

D. Note previously stated interests

50. **Effective management of transitions involves all of the following EXCEPT:**
    (Rigorous)

    A. Keeping students informed of the sequencing of instructional activities

    B. Using group fragmentation

    C. Changing the schedule frequently to maintain student interest

    D. Using academic transition signals

51. **What is most important to remember when assigning homework?**
    (Average)

    A. Homework should introduce new skills

    B. Homework should be assigned daily

    C. Homework should consist only of practice/review of skills previously introduced in class

    D. Homework should generally take less than thirty minutes to complete

52. **After Mrs. Cordova passed out an assignment, Jason loudly complained that he didn't want to do the assignment, laid his head on his desk, and refused to work when requested to do so. Mrs. Cordova ignored Jason and focused on the students who were working on the assignment. Jason eventually began to work on the assignment, at which time Mrs. Cordova approached his desk and praised him for working. What behavior management strategy was Mrs. Cordova implementing?**
    (Average)

    A. Proximity control

    B. Assertive discipline

    C. Token economy

    D. Planned ignoring

53. **There are students who are unmotivated in the learning environment because of learning problems they have experienced in the past. Some effective ways of helping a student become academically motivated include:**
    (Average)

    A. Setting goals for the student and expecting him to achieve them

    B. Avoiding giving immediate feedback, as it may be demoralizing to him

    C. Making sure the academic content relates to personal interests

    D. Planning subject matter based on grade level placement

54. **Sam did not turn in any homework on Tuesday or Wednesday morning. Sam's teacher said nothing about it until that Friday, at which time she told him he could not participate in the weekly free activity time because of his zeros in homework for the two days earlier that week. Which characteristic of an effective punisher was violated?**
    (Easy)

    A. Intensity

    B. Immediacy

    C. Contingency

    D. All of the above

55. **Which of the following is NOT a feature of effective classroom rules?**
    (Easy)

    A. They are about 4 to 6 in number

    B. They are negatively stated

    C. Consequences are consistent and immediate

    D. They can be tailored to individual teaching goals and teaching styles

56. **In establishing your behavior management plan with the students, it is best to:**
    (Average)

    A. Have rules written and in place on day one

    B. Hand out a copy of the rules to the students on day one

    C. Have separate rules for each class on day one

    D. Have students involved in creating the rules on day one

57. **Shyquan is in your inclusive class, and she exhibits a slower comprehension of assigned tasks and concepts. Her first two grades were Bs, but she is now receiving failing marks. She has seen the Resource Teacher. You should:**
(Rigorous)

    A. Ask for a review of current placement

    B. Tell Shyquan to seek extra help

    C. Ask Shyquan if she is frustrated

    D. Ask the regular education teacher to slow instruction

58. **The key to success for the exceptional student placed in a general education classroom is:**
(Easy)

    A. Access to the special aids and materials

    B. Support from the special education teacher

    C. Modification in the curriculum

    D. The general education teacher's belief that the student will profit from the placement

59. **Mrs. Freud is a consultant teacher. She has two students with Mr. Ricardo. Mrs. Freud should:**
(Rigorous)

    A. Co-teach

    B. Spend two days a week in the classroom helping out

    C. Discuss lessons with the teacher and suggest modifications before class

    D. Pull her students out for instructional modifications

60. **You should prepare for a parent-teacher conference by:**
(Average)

    A. Memorizing student progress/grades

    B. Anticipating questions

    C. Scheduling the meetings during your lunchtime

    D. Planning a tour of the school

61. **Acculturation refers to the individual's:**
(Rigorous)

    A. Gender

    B. Experiential background

    C. Social class

    D. Ethnic background

62. **To which aspect does fair assessment relate?**
    (Easy)

    A. Representation

    B. Acculturation

    C. Language

    D. All of the above

63. **A test that measures students' skill development in academic content areas is classified as an _____ test.**
    (Average)

    A. Achievement

    B. Aptitude

    C. Adaptive

    D. Intelligence

64. **Which of the following is an example of tactile perception?**
    (Average)

    A. Making an angel in the snow with one's body

    B. Running a specified course

    C. Identifying a rough surface with eyes closed

    D. Demonstrating aerobic exercises

65. **Which of the following activities best exemplifies a kinesthetic exercise in developing body awareness?**
    (Rigorous)

    A. Touching materials of different textures

    B. Playing a song/movement game like "Looby Loo"

    C. Identifying geometric shapes being drawn on one's back

    D. Making a shadow-box project

66. **Which of the following teaching activities is LEAST likely to enhance observational learning in students with special needs?**
    (Easy)

    A. A verbal description of the task to be performed, followed by having the children immediately attempt to perform the instructed behavior

    B. A demonstration of the behavior, followed by an immediate opportunity for the children to imitate the behavior

    C. A simultaneous demonstration and explanation of the behavior, followed by ample opportunity for the children to rehearse the instructed behavior

    D. Physically guiding the children through the behavior to be imitated, while verbally explaining the behavior

67. The _____ modality is most frequently used in the learning process.
    (Average)

    A. Auditory

    B. Visual

    C. Tactile

    D. All of the Above

68. Public Law 99-457 amended the EHA to make provisions for:
    (Easy)

    A. Education services for "uneducable" children

    B. Educational services for children in jail settings

    C. Special Education benefits for children birth to five years old

    D. Education services for medically fragile children

69. Some environmental elements that influence the effectiveness of learning styles include all EXCEPT:
    (Easy)

    A. Light

    B. Temperature

    C. Design

    D. Motivation

70. In order for a student to function independently in the learning environment, which of the following must be true?
    (Average)

    A. The learner must understand the nature of the content.

    B. The student must be able to do the assigned task.

    C. The teacher must communicate performance criteria to the learner.

    D. All of the above

71. What can a teacher plan that will allow him/her to avoid adverse situations with students?
    (Rigorous)

    A. Instructional techniques

    B. Instructional materials and formats

    C. Physical setting and the Environment

    D. All of the above

72. **John learns best through the auditory channel, so his teacher wants to reinforce his listening skills. Through which of the following types of equipment would instruction be most effectively presented?**
    (Easy)

    A. Overhead projector

    B. Audio recording device

    C. Microcomputer

    D. Opaque projector

73. **When teaching a student who is predominantly auditory to read, it is best to:**
    (Rigorous)

    A. Stress sight vocabulary

    B. Stress phonetic analysis

    C. Stress the shape and configuration of the word

    D. Stress rapid reading

74. **If a student is predominantly a visual learner, he may learn more effectively by:**
    (Easy)

    A. Reading aloud while studying

    B. Listening to a cassette tape

    C. Watching a video clip

    D. Using body movement

75. **A prerequisite skill is:**
    (Average)

    A. The lowest order skill in a hierarchy of skills needed to perform a specific task

    B. A skill that must be demonstrated before instruction on a specific task can begin

    C. A tool for accomplishing task analysis

    D. The smallest component of any skill

76. Under the provisions of IDEA, the student is entitled to all of these EXCEPT:
    (Easy)

    A. Placement in the best environment

    B. Placement in the least restrictive environment

    C. Provision of educational needs at no cost

    D. Provision of individualized, appropriate educational program

77. All of the following are suggestions for altering the presentation of tasks to match the student's rate of learning EXCEPT:
    (Average)

    A. Teach in several shorter segments of time rather than a single lengthy session.

    B. Continue to teach a task until the lesson is completed in order to provide more time on task.

    C. Watch for nonverbal cues that indicate students are becoming confused, bored, or restless.

    D. Avoid giving students an inappropriate amount of written work.

78. Which of the following is a good example of a generalization?
    (Rigorous)

    A. Jim has learned to add and is now ready to subtract.

    B. Sarah adds sets of units to obtain a product.

    C. Bill recognizes a vocabulary word on a billboard when traveling.

    D. Jane can spell the word "net" backwards to get the word "ten."

79. Students who recognize and name some letters, apply sounds to many of the consonants, and do some invented spelling, but do not recognize common spelling patterns are in which phase of learning to decode?
    (Average)

    A. Pre-alphabetic phase

    B. Partial alphabetic phase

    C. Full- alphabetic phase

    D. Consolidated alphabetic phase

80. The following words all describe an IEP objective EXCEPT:
    (Easy)

    A. Specific

    B. Observable

    C. Measurable

    D. Criterion-referenced

81. Alan has failed repeatedly in his academic work. He needs continuous feedback in order to experience small, incremental achievements. What type of instructional material would best meet this need?
    (Rigorous)

    A. Programmed materials

    B. Audiotapes

    C. Materials with no writing required

    D. Worksheets

82. After purchasing what seemed to be a very attractive new math kit for use with her students with SLD (specific learning disabilities), Ms. Davis discovered her students could not use the kit unless she read the math problems and instructions to them, as the readability level was higher than the majority of the students' functional reading capabilities. Which criterion of the materials selection did Ms. Davis most likely fail to consider when selecting this math kit?
    (Average)

    A. Durability

    B. Relevance

    C. Component parts

    D. Price

83. **Which of the following questions most directly evaluates the utility of instructional material?**
(Rigorous)

    A. Is the cost within budgetary means?

    B. Can the materials withstand handling by students?

    C. Are the materials organized in a useful manner?

    D. Are the needs of the students met by the use of the materials?

84. **A money bingo game was designed by Ms. Johnson for use with her middle grade students. Cards were constructed with different combinations of coins pasted on each of the nine spaces. Ms. Johnson called out various amounts of change (e.g., 30 cents), and students were instructed to cover the coin combinations on their cards, which equaled the amount of change (e.g., two dimes and two nickels, three dimes, and so on). The student who had the first bingo was required to add the coins in each of the spaces covered and tell the amounts before being declared the winner. Five of Ms. Johnson's sixth graders played the game during the ten-minute free activity time following math the first day the game was constructed. Which of the following attributes are present in this game in this situation?**
(Average)

    A. Accompanied by simple, uncomplicated rules

    B. Of brief duration, permitting replay

    C. Age appropriateness

    D. All of the above

85. According to the three tier RTI model, students who need a moderate amount of help in one of the five critical areas of reading instruction in a general education class would receive additional reading instruction through the: *(Average)*

    A. Core reading program

    B. Intensive Intervention program

    C. Modified Reading program

    D. Supplemental reading program

86. Modifications of course material may take the form of: *(Average)*

    A. Simplifying texts

    B. Parallel curriculum

    C. Taped textbooks

    D. All of the above

87. At which level of mathematics instruction will a child need to spend the most instructional and exploratory time in order to successfully master objectives? *(Average)*

    A. Symbolic Level

    B. Concept Level

    C. Mastery Level

    D. Connecting Level

88. Which of the following statements was NOT offered as a rationale for inclusion? *(Rigorous)*

    A. Special education students are not usually identified until their learning problems have become severe.

    B. Lack of funding will mean that support for the special needs children will not be available in the regular classroom.

    C. Putting children in segregated special education placements is stigmatizing.

    D. There are students with learning or behavior problems who do not meet special education requirements but who still need special services.

89. Janice requires occupational therapy and speech therapy services. She is your student. What must you do to insure her services are met? *(Rigorous)*

    A. Watch the services being rendered.

    B. Schedule collaboratively.

    C. Ask for services to be given in a push-in model.

    D. Ask them to train you to give the service.

90. What can you do to create a good working environment with a classroom assistant? *(Rigorous)*

    A. Plan lessons with the assistant.

    B. Write a contract that clearly defines his/her responsibilities in the classroom.

    C. Remove previously given responsibilities.

    D. All of the above

91. A paraprofessional has been assigned to assist you in the classroom. What action on the part of the teacher would lead to a poor working relationship? *(Average)*

    A. Having the paraprofessional lead a small group

    B. Telling the paraprofessional what you expect him/her to do

    C. Defining classroom behavior management as your responsibility alone

    D. Taking an active role in his/her evaluation

92. Jonathan has Attention Deficit Hyperactivity Disorder (ADHD). He is in a regular classroom and appears to be doing okay. However, his teacher does not want John in her class because he will not obey her when she asks him to stop doing a repetitive action such as tapping his foot. The teacher sees this as distracting during tests. John needs: *(Easy)*

    A. An IEP

    B. A 504 Plan

    C. A VESID evaluation

    D. A more restrictive environment

93. In which way is a computer like an effective teacher?
    (Average)

    A. Provides immediate feedback

    B. Sets the pace at the rate of the average student

    C. Produces records of errors made only

    D. Programs to skill levels at which students at respective chronological ages should be working

94. A Behavioral Intervention Plan (BIP):
    (Rigorous)

    A. Should be written by a team.

    B. Should be reviewed annually.

    C. Should be written by the teacher who is primarily responsible for the student.

    D. Should consider placement.

95. Bill talks out in class an average of 15 times an hour. Other youngsters sometimes talk out, but Bill does so at a higher:
    (Easy)

    A. Rate

    B. Intensity

    C. Volume

    D. Degree

96. Which category of behaviors would most likely be found on a behavior rating scale?
    (Easy)

    A. Disruptive, acting out

    B. Shy, withdrawn

    C. Aggressive (physical or verbal)

    D. All of the above

97. IDEA 2004 states that there are a disproportionate number of minority students classified as needing special education services. IDEA 2004 suggests that this is due to:
(Average)

   A. Socioeconomic status where disproportionate numbers exist

   B. Improper evaluations – Not making allowances for students who have English as a second language

   C. Growing population of minorities

   D. Percentage of drug abuse per ethnicity

98. Bob shows behavior problems like lack of attention, being out of his seat, and talking out. His teacher has kept data on these behaviors and has found that Bob is showing much better self-control since he has been self-managing himself through a behavior modification program. The most appropriate placement recommendation for Bob at this time is probably:
(Easy)

   A. Any available part-time special education program

   B. The regular classroom solely

   C. A behavior disorders resource room for one period a day

   D. A specific learning disabilities resource room for one period a day

99. A Behavior Intervention Plan (BIP) is based on the behaviorist assumption that many problem behaviors are:
(Average)

   A. Predictable

   B. Observed

   C. Conditioned

   D. Learned

100. Procedures employed to decrease targeted behaviors include:
(Rigorous)

    A. Punishment

    B. Negative reinforcement

    C. Shaping

    D. Both A and B

101. Target behaviors must be:
(Easy)

    A. Observable

    B. Measurable

    C. Definable

    D. All of the above

102. The most important step in writing a Functional Behavioral Assessment (FBA) is:
(Rigorous)

    A. Establish a replacement behavior.

    B. Establish levels of interventions.

    C. Establish antecedents related or causative to the behavior.

    D. Establish assessment periods of FBA effectiveness.

103. Which description best characterizes primary reinforcers of an edible nature?
(Average)

    A. Natural

    B. Unconditioned

    C. Innately motivating

    D. All of the above

104. Mrs. Chang is trying to prevent satiation from occurring so that her reinforcers will be effective, as she is using a continuous reinforcement schedule. Which of the following ideas would be LEAST effective in preventing satiation?
(Rigorous)

    A. Use only one type of edible rather than a variety.

    B. Ask for ten vocabulary words rather than twenty.

    C. Give pieces of cereal, bits of fruit, or M&Ms rather than large portions of edibles.

    D. Administer a peanut then a sip of water.

105. **Which tangible reinforcer would Mr. Whiting find to be MOST effective with teenagers?**
(Easy)

   A. Plastic whistle

   B. Winnie-the-Pooh book

   C. Poster of a current rock star

   D. Toy ring

106. **A positive reinforcer is generally effective if it is desired by the student and is:**
(Easy)

   A. Worthwhile in size

   B. Given immediately after the desired behavior

   C. Given only upon the occurrence of the target behavior

   D. All of the above

107. **Dispensing school supplies is a component associated with which type of reinforcement system?**
(Average)

   A. Activity reinforcement

   B. Tangible reinforcement

   C. Token reinforcement

   D. Both B and C

108. **Which type of reinforcement system is most easily generalized into other settings?**
(Average)

   A. Social reinforcement

   B. Activity reinforcement

   C. Tangible reinforcement

   D. Token reinforcement

109. NCLB and IDEA 2004 changed special education teacher requirements by:
 (Easy)

   A. Requiring a highly-qualified status for job placement

   B. Adding changes to the requirement for certifications

   C. Adding legislation requiring teachers to maintain knowledge of law

   D. Requiring inclusive environmental experience prior to certification

110. In the Grammatic Closure subtest of the Illinois Test of Psycholinguistic Abilities, the child is presented with a picture representing statements such as the following: "Here is one die; here are two ____." This test is essentially a test of:
 (Rigorous)

   A. Phonology

   B. Syntax

   C. Morphology

   D. Semantics

111. Which law specifically states that, "Full Inclusion is not the only way for a student to reach his/her highest potential"?
 (Rigorous)

   A. IDEA

   B. IDEA 97

   C. IDEA 2004

   D. Part 200

112. Which of the following is untrue about the ending "er" ?
 (Rigorous)

   A. It is an example of a free morpheme.

   B. It represents one of the smallest units of meaning within a word.

   C. It is called an inflectional ending.

   D. When added to a word, it connotes a comparative status.

113. **NCLB (No Child Left Behind Act) was signed on January 8, 2002. It addresses what?**
(Rigorous)

   A. Accessibility of curriculum to the student

   B. Administrative incentives for school improvements

   C. The funding to provide services required

   D. Accountability of school personnel for student achievement

114. **The social skills of students in intellectual disabilities programs are likely to be appropriate for children of their mental age, rather than chronological age. This means that the teacher will need to do all of the following EXCEPT:**
(Easy)

   A. Model desired behavior.

   B. Provide clear instructions.

   C. Expect age-appropriate behaviors.

   D. Adjust the physical environment when necessary.

115. **Which of the following is a language disorder?**
(Average)

   A. Articulation problems

   B. Stuttering

   C. Aphasia

   D. Excessive Nasality

116. **Which of the following is a speech disorder?**
(Average)

   A. Disfluency

   B. Aphasia

   C. Delayed language

   D. Comprehension difficulties

117. **Which of the following is an example of cross-modal perception involving integrating visual stimuli to an auditory verbal process?**
(Rigorous)

   A. Following spoken directions

   B. Describing a picture

   C. Finding certain objects in pictures

   D. Both B and C

118. Matthew's conversational speech is adequate, but when he tries to speak before a group of more than two listeners, his speech becomes mumbling and halting. Which of the following activities would be LEAST helpful in strengthening Matthew's self-expression skills? *(Rigorous)*

   A. Having him participate in show-and-tell time

   B. Asking him comprehension questions about a story that was read to the class

   C. Having him recite a poem in front of the class, with two other children

   D. Asking him to tell a joke to the rest of the class

119. All of the modes listed below are primary categories of Augmentative Alternative Communication EXCEPT: *(Easy)*

   A. Wheelchairs

   B. Graphical communication boards

   C. Eye gaze techniques

   D. Sign language

120. A functional curriculum includes: *(Average Rigor)*

   A. Regents curriculum

   B. Life skills

   C. Remedial academics

   D. Vocational placement

PRAXIS Special Education Practice Test Kit
Post-Test Sample Questions with Rationales

1. Howard has been diagnosed as having maladaptive behavior of an immature/anxious withdrawn nature. A behavior that we might expect of Howard, considering his diagnosis is:
   (Rigorous)

   A. Resistance

   B. Teasing

   C. Fantasizing

   D. Hostility

Answer: C. Fantasizing
Choices A, B, and D are traits of aggressive, acting-out behavior. Choice C, however, is the trait of anxious, withdrawn behavior.

2. Which of these is listed as only a minor scale on the Behavior Problem Checklist?
   (Average)

   A. Motor Excess

   B. Conduct Disorder

   C. Socialized Aggression

   D. Anxiety/Withdrawal

Answer: A. Motor Excess
Motor Excess has to do with over activity, or hyperactivity, in physical movement. The other three items are disorders, all of which may be characterized by excessive activity.

3. Kenny, a fourth grader, has trouble comprehending analogies, using comparative, spatial, and temporal words, and multiple meanings. Language interventions for Kenny would focus on:
   (Rigorous)

   A. Morphology

   B. Syntax

   C. Pragmatics

   D. Semantics

Answer: D. Semantics
Semantics has to do with word meanings. Semantic tests measure receptive and expressive vocabulary skills.

4. Five-year-old Tom continues to substitute the "w" sound for the "r" sound when pronouncing words; therefore, he often distorts words e.g., "wabbit" for "rabbit" and "wat" for "rat." His articulation disorder is basically a problem in:
   (Rigorous)

   A. Phonology

   B. Morphology

   C. Syntax

   D. Semantics

Answer: A. Phonology

- Morphology is the study of the structure of words and the rules for combining morphemes into words.
- Syntax refers to the set of rules that govern sentence formation and the speaker's understanding of the structure of phrases and sentences.
- Assessment of morphology refers to linguistic structure of words.
- Assessment of syntax includes grammatical usage of word classes, word order, and transformational rules for the variance of word order.

5. The Carrow Elicited Language Inventory is a test designed to give the examiner diagnostic information about a child's expressive grammatical competence. Which of the following language components is being assessed?
(Rigorous)

    A.   Phonology

    B.   Morphology

    C.   Syntax

    D.   Both B and C

Answer: C. Syntax

- Morphology is the study of the structure of words and the rules for combining morphemes into words.
- Syntax refers to the set of rules that govern sentence formation and the speaker's understanding of the structure of phrases and sentences.
- Assessment of morphology refers to linguistic structure of words.
- Assessment of syntax includes grammatical usage of word classes, word order, and transformational rules for the variance of word order.

6. **At what stage of cognitive development might we expect a student to being to think about and systematically consider possible future goals?**
(Average)

    A.   Early Adolescence

    B.   Middle Adolescence

    C.   Late Adolescence

    D.   Adulthood

Answer: C. Late Adolescence
With some experience in using more complex thinking processes, the focus of middle adolescence often expands to include more philosophical and futuristic concerns, including the following:

- Often questions more extensively.
- Often analyzes more extensively.
- Thinks about and begins to form a code of ethics.
- Thinks about different possibilities and begins to develop own identity.
- Thinks about and begins to systematically consider possible future goals.
- Thinks about and begins to make his or her own plans.
- Begins to think long term.
- Systematic thinking begins to influence relationships with others.

7. **Which of the following manifestations can be characteristic of students placed in the exceptionality category of Other Health Impaired?**
   (Average)

   A. Limited strength, vitality, or alertness

   B. Severe communication and developmental problems

   C. Chronic or acute health problems

   D. All of the above

Answer: D. All of the above
Other Health Impaired means having limited strength, vitality, or alertness, due to chronic or acute health problems such as a heart condition, tuberculosis, rheumatic fever, nephritis, asthma, sickle cell anemia, hemophilia, epilepsy, lead poisoning, leukemia, or diabetes, which adversely affects a child's educational performance.

8. **A developmental delay may be indicated by a:**
   (Rigorous)

   A. Second grader having difficulty buttoning clothing

   B. Stuttered response

   C. Kindergartner not having complete bladder control

   D. Withdrawn behavior

Answer: A. Second grader having difficulty buttoning clothing
Buttoning of clothing is generally mastered by the age of 4. While many children have full bladder control by age 4, it is not unusual for "embarrassing accidents" to occur.

9. Which is *least* indicative of a developmental delay?
   (Rigorous)

   A. Deficits in language and speech production

   B. Deficits in gross motor skills

   C. Deficits in self-help skills

   D. Deficits in arithmetic computation skills

Answer: D. Deficits in arithmetic computation skills
Arithmetic computation is a specific, learned skill. Developmental delay is a term used for a delay or deficit that is present in many or most cognitive and adaptive areas, not just one academic skill. In a pre-school environment, disabling conditions consistent with a developmental delay are manifested as inability to learn adequate readiness skills, to demonstrate self-help, adaptive, social-interpersonal, communication, or gross motor skills. The most typical symptoms exhibited by school-age students are inattention to tasks, disruptiveness, inability to learn to read, write, spell, or perform mathematical computations, unintelligible speech, an appearance of not being able to see or hear adequately, frequent daydreaming, excessive movement, and, in general, clumsiness and ineptitude in most school-related activities.

10. An organic reason for mild learning and behavioral disabilities is:
    (Rigorous)

    A. Inadequate education

    B. Toxins

    C. Biochemical factors

    D. Nutrition

Answer: B. Toxins
Causes for disabilities can primarily be divided into two major categories: organic (biological) and environmental. Under the organic category, prenatal, perinatal, and postnatal factors, genetic factors, biochemical factors, and maturational lag are listed. These are contributors that originate within the body (endogenous).

11. **Of the various factors that contribute to delinquency and anti-social behavior, which has been found to be the weakest?**
    (Rigorous)

    A. Criminal behavior and/or alcoholism in the father

    B. Lax mother and punishing father

    C. Socioeconomic disadvantage

    D. Long history of broken home and marital discord among parents

Answer: C. Socioeconomic disadvantage
There are many examples of choices A, B, and D, where there is socioeconomic advantage.

12. **Criteria for choosing behaviors to measure by frequency include all but those that:**
    (Easy)

    A. Have an observable beginning

    B. Last a long time

    C. Last a short time

    D. Occur often

Answer: B. Last a long time
We use frequency to measure behaviors that do not last a long time. Measures that extend over a long period are better measured by duration.

13. Ryan is three and her temper tantrums last for an hour. Bryan is eight and he does not stay on task for more than ten minutes without teacher prompts. These behaviors differ from normal children in terms of their:
(Average)

    A. Rate

    B. Topography

    C. Duration

    D. Magnitude

Answer: C. Duration
Duration is the length of time a particular behavior continues. Duration is measured by timing the behavior from start to finish.

14. The most direct method of obtaining assessment data, and perhaps the most objective, is:
(Easy)

    A. Testing

    B. Self-recording

    C. Observation

    D. Experimenting

Answer: C. Observation
Observation is often better than testing, due to language, culture, or other factors.

15. **The most important member of the transition team is the:**
    (Easy)

    A. Parent

    B. Student

    C. Secondary personnel

    D. Postsecondary personnel

Answer: B. Student
Transition planning is a student-centered event that necessitates a collaborative endeavor. Responsibilities are shared by the student, parents, secondary personnel, and postsecondary personnel, who are all members of the transition team; however, it is important that the student play a key role in transition planning. This will entail asking the student to identify preferences and interests and to attend meetings on transition planning. The degree of success experienced by the student in postsecondary educational settings depends on the student's degree of motivation, independence, self-direction, self-advocacy, and academic abilities developed in high school. Student participation in transition activities should be implemented as early as possible and no later than age 16.

16. **Echolalia is a characteristic of which disability?**
    (Average)

    A. Autism

    B. Intellectual disabilities

    C. Social Pragmatic Disorder

    D. ADHD

Answer: A. Autism
Echolalia is echoing/repeating the speech of others, which is a characteristic of autism.

17. **Satisfaction of the LRE requirement means:**
(Easy)

   A. The school is providing the best services it can offer.

   B. The school is providing the best services the district has to offer.

   C. The student is being educated with the fewest special education services necessary.

   D. The student is being educated in the least restrictive setting that meets his or her needs.

Answer: D. The student is being educated in the least restrictive setting that meets his or her needs.

The legislation mandates LRE (Least Restrictive Environment). The specifics of what environment constitutes "least restrictive" will vary depending upon each child's needs.

18. **IDEA specified that students with disabilities must be placed in the Least Restrictive Environment (LRE). In the Cascade System of Special Education Services, which of the following would be considered the LRE for a student with a mild learning disability?**
(Easy)

   A. A Co-Teach setting

   B. Paraprofessional support in the general education classroom

   C. A separate special education classroom

   D. There is not enough information to make that determination

Answer: D. There is not enough information to make that determination
Although choices A, B, or C could provide LRE for some students, decisions must be made according to individual student need, not a disability condition. More information about the student is needed to be able to specify what the student needs and how services can be delivered in the Least Restrictive Environment appropriate to the needs of the individual student.

19. **Vocational training programs are based on all of the following ideas EXCEPT:**
    (Average)

    A. Students obtain career training from elementary through high school.

    B. Students acquire specific training in job skills prior to exiting school.

    C. Students need specific training and supervision in applying skills learned in school to requirements in job situations.

    D. Students obtain needed instruction and field-based experiences that help them to be able to work in specific occupations.

Answer: A. Students obtain career training from elementary through high school.
Vocational education programs or transition programs prepare students for entry into the labor force. They are usually incorporated into the work-study at the high school or post-secondary levels. They are usually focused on job skills, job opportunities, skill requirements for specific jobs, personal qualifications in relation to job requirements, work habits, money management, and academic skills needed for specific jobs.

20. **IDEA identifies specific disability conditions under which students may be eligible to receive special education services. Of the following, which is NOT a specific disability area identified in IDEA?**
    (Average)

    A. Other Health Impairment

    B. Emotional Disturbance

    C. Specific Learning Disability

    D. Attention Deficit Disorder

Answer: D. Attention Deficit Disorder
Attention Deficit Disorder is not a separate disability area in IDEA. Students with ADD/ADHD may qualify for special education services under the Other Health Impairment area, if the disability is significant enough to require special education support. Many students with ADD/ADHD receive services through 504; some require no additional support at all.

21. To be entitled to protection under Section 504, the individual must meet the definition of a person with a disability, which is any person who: 1. has a physical or mental impairment that substantially limits one or more of such person's major life activities, 2. has a record of such impairment, or 3. is regarded as having such impairment. Which of the following is considered a "major life activity"?
(Easy)

    A. Engaging in sports, hobbies, and recreation

    B. Caring for oneself

    C. Driving a car

    D. Having a social network

Answer: C. Driving a car
Major life activities include caring for oneself, performing manual tasks, walking, seeing, hearing, speaking, breathing, learning, and working. While the others may be important to one's quality of life, they are not considered major life activities under 504.

22. NCLB and IDEA 2004 changed Special Education Teacher requirements by:
(Easy)

    A. Requiring a Highly Qualified status for job placement

    B. Adding changes to the requirement for certifications

    C. Adding legislation requiring teachers to maintain knowledge of law

    D. Requiring inclusive environmental experience prior to certification

Answer: A. Requiring a Highly Qualified status for job placement
NCLB and IDEA 2004 place a requirement that all teachers shall be highly qualified to teach in the content areas they teach.

23. Hector is a 10th grader in a program for students with severe emotional disturbances. After a classmate taunted him about his mother, Hector threw a desk at the other boy and attacked him. A crisis intervention team tried to break up the fight, and one teacher hurt his knee. The other boy received a concussion. Hector now faces disciplinary measures. How long can he be suspended without the suspension constituting a "change of placement"?
(Rigorous)

    A.   5 days

    B.   10 days

    C.   10 + 30 days

    D.   60 days

Answer: B. 10 days
According to *Honig versus Doe*, 1988, where the student has presented an immediate threat to others, that student may be temporarily suspended for up to ten school days to give the school and the parents time to review the IEP and discuss possible alternatives to the current placement.

24. *Irving Independent School District v Tatro, 1984* **is significant in its impact upon what component of the delivery of special education services?**
(Average)

- A. Health Services
- B. FAPE
- C. Speech Therapy
- D. LRE

Answer: A. Health Services
IDEA lists health services as one of the related services that schools are mandated to provide to exceptional students. Amber Tatro, who had spina bifida, required the insertion of a catheter on a regular schedule in order to empty her bladder. The issue was specifically over the classification of clean, intermittent catheterization (CIC) as a medical service (not covered under IDEA) or a related health service, which would be covered. In this instance, the catheterization was not declared a medical service, but a related service necessary for the student to have in order to benefit from special education. The school district was obliged to provide the service. The Tatro case has implications for students with other medical impairments who may need services to allow them to attend classes at the school.

25. The family plays a vital role in our society by:
(Easy)

- A. Assuming a protective and nurturing function
- B. Acting as the primary unit for social control
- C. Playing a major role in the transmission of cultural values and morals
- D. All of the above

Answer: D. All of the above
The family is the primary influence in all the roles listed.

26. **The first American school for students who are deaf was founded in 1817 by:**
    (Easy)

    A. Jean Marc Itard

    B. Thomas Hopkins Gallaudet

    C. Dorothea Dix

    D. Maria Montessori

Answer: B. Thomas Hopkins Gallaudet
In 1817, Thomas Hopkins Gallaudet founded the first American school for students who were deaf, known today as Gallaudet College in Washington, D.C.

27. **The movement towards serving as many children with disabilities as possible in the regular classroom with supports and services grew out of:**
    (Average)

    A. The Full Service Model

    B. The Regular Education Model

    C. The Normalization movement

    D. The Mainstream Model

Answer: C. The Normalization movement
The Normalization movement advocated movement toward less restrictive environments for people with disabilities. It led to deinstitutionalization and the attempt to let people with disabilities live, go to school, and work in an environment as "normal" or as close as possible to that of their peer group without disabilities.

28. In successful inclusion:
(Easy)

    A.   A variety of instructional arrangements is available

    B.   School personnel shift the responsibility for learning outcomes to the student

    C.   The physical facilities are used as they are

    D.   Regular classroom teachers have sole responsibility for evaluating student progress

Answer: A. A variety of instructional arrangements is available
Some support systems and activities that are in evidence where successful inclusion has occurred:

Attitudes and beliefs
- The regular teacher believes the student can succeed.
- School personnel are committed to accepting responsibility for the learning outcomes of students with disabilities.
- School personnel and the students in the class have been prepared to receive a student with disabilities

Services and physical accommodations
- Services needed by the student are available (e.g. health, physical, occupational, or speech therapy).
- Accommodations to the physical plant and equipment are adequate to meet the students' needs (e.g. toys, building and playground facilities, learning materials, assistive devices).

School support
- The principal understands the needs of students with disabilities.
- Adequate numbers of personnel, including aides and support personnel, are available.
- Adequate staff development and technical assistance, based on the needs of the school personnel, are being provided (e.g. information on disabilities, instructional methods, awareness and acceptance activities for students and team-building skills).
- Appropriate policies and procedures for monitoring individual student progress, including grading and testing are in place.

Collaboration
- Special educators are part of the instructional or planning team.
- Teaming approaches are used for program implementation and problem solving.

- Regular teachers, special education teachers, and other specialists collaborate (e.g. co-teach, team teach, work together on teacher assistance teams).

Instructional methods
- Teachers have the knowledge and skills needed to select and adapt curricular and instructional methods according to individual student needs.
- A variety of instructional arrangements is available (e.g. team teaching, cross-grade grouping, peer tutoring, teacher assistance teams).
- Teachers foster a cooperative learning environment and promote socialization.

29. **Teaching children functional skills that will be useful in their home life and neighborhoods is the basis of:**
    (Rigorous)

    A. Curriculum-based instruction

    B. Community-based instruction

    C. Transition planning

    D. Functional curriculum

Answer: B. Community-based instruction
Teaching functional skills in the wider curriculum is considered Community-based instruction.

30. **The transition activities that have to be addressed, unless the IEP team finds it uncalled for, include all of the following EXCEPT:**
    (Rigorous)

    A. Instruction

    B. Volunteer opportunities

    C. Community experiences

    D. Development of objectives related to employment and other post-school areas

Answer: B. Volunteer opportunities
Volunteer opportunities, although worthwhile, are not listed as one of the three transition activities that have to be addressed on a student's IEP.

31. Which learning theory emphasizes at least seven different ways in which a student learns?
    (Average)

    A. Cognitive Approach

    B. Ecological Approach

    C. Multiple Intelligences

    D. Brain Based Learning

Answer: C. Multiple Intelligences
The Multiple Intelligence Theory, developed by Howard Gardner, suggests that students learn in (at least) seven different ways: visually/spatially, musically, verbally, logically /mathematically, interpersonally, intrapersonally, and bodily/kinesthetically.

32. According to Piaget's theory, a normally developing third grader would be at what stage of development?
    (Average)

    A. Sensory motor

    B. Pre-Operational

    C. Concrete Operational

    D. Formal Operational

Answer: B. Pre-Operational
Piaget's observations about stages of development have implications for both theories of learning and strategies for teaching. Piaget recorded observations on the following four learning stages: sensory motor stage (from birth to age 2); pre-operational stages (ages 2–7 or early elementary); concrete operational (ages 7–11 or upper elementary); and formal operational (ages 7–15 or late elementary/high school). Piaget believed children passed through this series of stages to develop from the most basic forms of concrete thinking to sophisticated levels of abstract thinking.

33. The components that must be included in the written notice provided to parents prior to a proposal or refusal to initiate or make a change in the child's identification, evaluation, or educational placement are: 1. A listing of parental due process safeguards; 2. A description and a rationale for the chosen action; 3. Assurance that the language and content of the notices were understood by the parents; and 4. _____.

(Rigorous)

    A.   A detailed listing of components that were the basis for the decision

    B.   A detailed listing of the Related Services provided by Special Education

    C.   A list of the disability areas covered by IDEA

    D.   The telephone numbers of local attorneys who specialize in education law

Answer: A. A detailed listing of components that were the basis for the decision

Written notice must be provided to parents prior to a proposal or refusal to initiate or make a change in the child's identification, evaluation, or educational placement. Notices must contain:

- A listing of parental due process safeguards
- A description and a rationale for the chosen action
- A detailed listing of components (e.g., tests, records, reports) that were the basis for the decision
- Assurance that the language and content of the notices were understood by the parents

34. **What is MOST descriptive of vocational training in special education? (Easy)**

    A. Trains students in intellectual disabilities solely.

    B. Segregates students with and without disabilities in vocational training programs.

    C. Only includes students capable of moderate supervision.

    D. Instruction focuses upon self-help skills, social-interpersonal skills, motor skills, rudimentary academic skills, simple occupational skills, and lifetime leisure and occupational skills

Answer: D. Instruction focuses upon self-help skills, social-interpersonal skills, motor skills, rudimentary academic skills, simple occupational skills, and lifetime leisure and occupational skills.

Persons with disabilities are mainstreamed with non-disabled students where possible. Special sites provide training for those persons with more severe disabilities who are unable to be successfully taught in an integrated setting. Specially-trained vocational counselors monitor and supervise student work sites.

35. **A best practice for evaluating student performance and progress on IEPs is:**
    (Rigorous)

    A. Formal assessment

    B. Curriculum-based assessment

    C. Criterion-based assessment

    D. Norm-referenced evaluation

Answer: C. Criterion-based assessment
Criterion referenced tests measure a student's knowledge of specific content, usually related to classroom instruction. The student's performance is compared to a set of criteria or a pre-established standard of information the student is expected to know. On these tests, what the student knows is more important than how he or she compares to other students. Examples include math quizzes at the end of a chapter, or some state mandated tests of specific content. Criterion referenced tests are used to determine whether a student has mastered required skills (criteria). As such, they are most appropriate for assessing whether a student has mastered the objectives on an IEP.

36. **Who is responsible for the implementation of a student's IEP?**
    (Easy)

    A. Related Service Providers

    B. General Education Teacher

    C. Special Education Teacher

    D. All of the Above

Answer: D. All of the above
The Special Education teacher may be the person responsible for writing, distributing, and monitoring progress on the IEP, but all teachers and staff who interact with a child on an IEP are required to follow the dictates of the IEP.

37. **The components of effective lesson plan include: quizzes, or review of the previous lesson, step-by-step presentations with multiple examples, guided practice and feedback, and _____.**
    (Average)

    A. hands-on projects

    B. manipulative materials

    C. audio-visual aids

    D. independent practice

Answer: D. independent practice
While choices A, B, and C may be written into a lesson plan to supplement any lesson, independent practice that requires the student to produce faster, increasingly independent (reduced scaffolding) responses should be a key component of every lesson plan.

38. The minimum number of IEP meetings required per year is:
(Average)

    A.   As many as necessary

    B.   One

    C.   Two

    D.   Three

Answer: B. One
P. L. 99-457 (1986) grants an annual IEP.

39. Which of these groups is not comprehensively covered by IDEA?
(Average)

    A.   Gifted and talented

    B.   People with intellectual disabilities

    C.   Specific learning disabilities

    D.   People with speech and language impairments

Answer: A. Gifted and talented
The Individuals with Disabilities Education Act, 101-476 (1990), did not cover all exceptional children. It did not address the needs of gifted students. The Gifted and Talented Children's Act, P. L. 95-56, was passed in 1978.

40. **Which of the following is NOT an appropriate assessment modification or accommodation for a student with a learning disability?**
    (Average)

    A. Having the test read orally to the student

    B. Writing down the student's dictated answers

    C. Allowing the student to take the assessment home to complete

    D. Extending the time for the student to take the assessment

Answer: C. Allowing the student to take the assessment home to complete
Unless a student is homebound, the student should take assessments in class or in another classroom setting. All the other items listed are appropriate accommodations.

41. **Larry has a moderate intellectual disability. He will probably do best in a classroom that has:**
    (Average)

    A. A reduced class size

    B. A structured learning schedule

    C. Use of hands-on concrete learning materials and experiences

    D. All of the above

Answer: D. All of the above
Depending on the individual needs of the student, all three classroom characteristics could be appropriate.

42. **A consultant teacher should be meeting the needs of his/her students by:**
    (Easy)

    A. Pushing in to do small-group instruction with regular education students

    B. Asking the student to show his/her reasoning for failing

    C. Meeting with the teacher before class to discuss adaptations and expectations

    D. Accompanying the student to class

Answer: A. Pushing in to do small-group instruction with regular education students
Students that receive consult services are receiving minimum instructional services. They require little modification to their educational program, and these modifications should take place in the general education classroom.

43. **Which assistive device can be used by those who are visually impaired to assist in their learning?**
    (Rigorous)

    A. Soniguide

    B. Personal Companion

    C. Closed Circuit Television (CCTV)

    D. ABVI

Answer: C. Closed Circuit Television (CCTV)
CCTV is used to enlarge material such as worksheets and books so that it can appear in a readable size.

44. Marisol has been mainstreamed into a ninth grade language arts class. Although her behavior is satisfactory, and she likes the class, Marisol's reading level is about two years below grade level. The class has been assigned to read *Great Expectations* and write a report. What intervention would be LEAST successful in helping Marisol complete this assignment?
(Average)

   A. Having Marisol listen to a taped recording while following the story in the regular text

   B. Giving her a modified version of the story

   C. Telling her to choose a different book that she can read

   D. Showing a film to the entire class and comparing and contrasting it with the book

Answer: C. Telling her to choose a different book that she can read
Choices A, B, and D are positive interventions. Choice C is not an intervention that lets her access the same curriculum as her peers.

45. Educators who advocate educating all children in their neighborhood classrooms and schools, who propose the end of labeling and segregation of special needs students in special classes, and who call for the delivery of special supports and services directly in the classroom, may be said to support the:
(Rigorous)

   A. Full service model

   B. Regular education initiative

   C. Full inclusion model

   D. Mainstream model

Answer: C. Full inclusion model
Advocates of the full inclusion model believe all students must be included in the regular classroom.

46. The Peabody Individual Achievement Test (PIAT) is an individually administered test. It measures math, decoding, comprehension, spelling, and general information, and reports comparison scores. Data is offered on standardization, validity, reliability, and so on. This achievement test has features of a:
(Rigorous)

   A.   Norm-Referenced Test

   B.   Diagnostic Test

   C.   Screening Tool

   D.   A and C

Answer: D. A and C
Norm-referenced tests compare students with others of his age or grade. It can be used for screening or placement of students.

47. Support can be given for all but which of the following facts? IQ scores:
(Rigorous)

   A.   Are interchangeable but not necessarily consistent between tests of intelligence

   B.   Can fluctuate over time periods

   C.   Measure innate intelligence

   D.   Are single elements of the total abilities attributable to an individual

Answer: C. Measure innate intelligence
IQ scores:
- Do not measure innate intelligence
- Are variable and can change
- Are only estimates of ability
- Reflect only a part of the spectrum of human abilities
- Are not necessarily consistent from test to test
- Are just one sample of behavior, therefore they do not give us all the essential information needed about a student

48. Which of these would be the least effective measure of behavioral disorders?
(Easy)

- A. Projective test
- B. Ecological assessment
- C. Achievement test
- D. Psychodynamic analysis

Answer: C. Achievement test
An achievement test measures mastery of specific skills. The other tests measure behavior and emotional adjustment.

49. Anecdotal Records should:
(Average)

- A. Record observable behavior
- B. End with conjecture
- C. Record motivational factors
- D. Note previously stated interests.

Answer: A. Record observable behavior
Anecdotal records should only record observable behavior, describing the actions and not inferences about possible interest or motivational factors that may lead to prejudicial reviews.

50. **Effective management of transitions involves all of the following EXCEPT:**
    (Rigorous)

    A. Keeping students informed of the sequencing of instructional activities

    B. Using group fragmentation

    C. Changing the schedule frequently to maintain student interest

    D. Using academic transition signals

Answer: C. Changing the schedule frequently to maintain student interest
While you do want to use a variety of activities to maintain student interest, changing the schedule too frequently will result in loss of instructional time due to unorganized transitions. Effective teachers manage transitions from one activity to another in a systematically oriented way through efficient management of instructional matter, sequencing of instructional activities, moving students in groups and by employing academic transition signals. Through an efficient use of class time, achievement is increased because students spend more class time engaged in on-task behavior. These principles are doubly important when working with some learning disabilities.

51. **What is most important to remember when assigning homework?**
    (Average)

    A. Homework should introduce new skills

    B. Homework should be assigned daily

    C. Homework should consist only of practice/review of skills previously introduced in class

    D. Homework should generally take less than thirty minutes to complete

Answer: C. Homework should consist only of practice/review of skills previously introduced in class
The purpose of homework is to practice/review skills previously introduced in class. Homework should never introduce new skills.

52. After Mrs. Cordova passed out an assignment, Jason loudly complained that he didn't want to do the assignment, laid his head on his desk, and refused to work when requested to do so. Mrs. Cordova ignored Jason and focused on the students who were working on the assignment. Jason eventually began to work on the assignment, at which time Mrs. Cordova approached his desk and praised him for working. What behavior management strategy was Mrs. Cordova implementing?
(Average)

    A.   Proximity control

    B.   Assertive discipline

    C.   Token economy

    D.   Planned ignoring

Answer: D. Planned ignoring
Mrs. Cordova is using planned ignoring. Planned ignoring means the teacher determines that an inappropriate behavior will be ignored. This often works with attention seeking behaviors. In the ideal situation, once the attention is removed the behavior ceases. It is important, however, to ensure that the student has other more appropriate behavioral options for getting the needed attention available and that the teacher notices them, too.

53. There are students who are unmotivated in the learning environment because of learning problems they have experienced in the past. Some effective ways of helping a student become academically motivated include:
(Average)

    A. Setting goals for the student and expecting him to achieve them

    B. Avoiding giving immediate feedback, as it may be demoralizing to him

    C. Making sure the academic content relates to personal interests

    D. Planning subject matter based on grade level placement

Answer: C. Making sure the academic content relates to personal interests
A student who is unmotivated in a conventional setting may become interested in learning through an individualized program. In such a setting, he can make choices, learn in accordance with his preferred learning style, and participate in pairs or groups, as well as by himself at his own pace.

54. Sam did not turn in any homework on Tuesday or Wednesday morning. Sam's teacher said nothing about it until that Friday, at which time she told him he could not participate in the weekly free activity time because of his zeros in homework for the two days earlier that week. Which characteristic of an effective punisher was violated?
(Easy)

    A. Intensity

    B. Immediacy

    C. Contingency

    D. All of the above

Answer: B. Immediacy
Immediacy was violated, as the punishment was meted out two days after its occurrence. This lapse in time might have rendered it useless or ineffective.

55. Which of the following is NOT a feature of effective classroom rules?
(Easy)

   A.   They are about 4 to 6 in number

   B.   They are negatively stated

   C.   Consequences are consistent and immediate

   D.   They can be tailored to individual teaching goals and teaching styles

Answer: B. They are negatively stated
Rules should be positively stated, and they should follow the other three features listed.

56. In establishing your behavior management plan with the students, it is best to:
(Average)

   A.   Have rules written and in place on day one

   B   Hand out a copy of the rules to the students on day one

   C.   Have separate rules for each class on day one

   D.   Have students involved in creating the rules on day one

Answer: D. Have students involved in creating the rules on day one
Students are more apt to follow rules when they know the reasons they are in place and took part in creating them. It may be good to already have a few rules pre-written and then discuss whether they cover all the rules the students have created. If not, it is possible you may want to modify your set of pre-written rules.

57. **Shyquan is in your inclusive class, and she exhibits a slower comprehension of assigned tasks and concepts. Her first two grades were Bs, but she is now receiving failing marks. She has seen the Resource Teacher. You should:**
(Rigorous)

   A. Ask for a review of current placement

   B. Tell Shyquan to seek extra help

   C. Ask Shyquan if she is frustrated

   D. Ask the regular education teacher to slow instruction

Answer: A. Ask for a review of current placement
All of the responses listed above can be deemed correct, but you are responsible for reviewing her ability to function in the inclusive environment. Shyquan may or may not know she is not grasping the work, and she has sought out extra help with the Resource Teacher. Also, if the regular education class students are successful, the class should not be slowed to adjust to Shyquan's learning rate. It is more likely that she may require a more modified curriculum to stay on task and to succeed academically. This would require a more restrictive environment.

58. **The key to success for the exceptional student placed in a general education classroom is:**
(Easy)

   A. Access to the special aids and materials

   B. Support from the special education teacher

   C. Modification in the curriculum

   D. The general education teacher's belief that the student will profit from the placement

Answer: D. The general education teacher's belief that the student will profit from the placement
All personnel involved with the student must maintain a positive attitude about the success of the student in the general education program. A teacher who has a negative attitude is less likely to provide the appropriate accommodations for the student.

59. Mrs. Freud is a consultant teacher. She has two students with Mr. Ricardo. Mrs. Freud should:
(Rigorous)

    A.   Co-teach

    B.   Spend two days a week in the classroom helping out

    C.   Discuss lessons with the teacher and suggest modifications before class

    D.   Pull her students out for instructional modifications

Answer: C. Discuss lessons with the teacher and suggest modifications before class
Consultant teaching provides the minimum intervention possible for the academic success of the child. Pushing in or pulling out are not essential components. However, an occasional observation as a classroom observer who does not single out any students may also be helpful in providing modifications for the student.

60. You should prepare for a parent-teacher conference by:
(Average)

    A.   Memorizing student progress/grades

    B.   Anticipating questions

    C.   Scheduling the meetings during your lunchtime

    D.   Planning a tour of the school

Answer: B. Anticipating questions
It pays to anticipate parent questions, so you will more likely to be able to appropriately answer the questions. Anticipating the questions the parents may ask can help you plan to topics that need to be addressed in the conference.

61. Acculturation refers to the individual's:
    (Rigorous)

    A. Gender

    B. Experiential background

    C. Social class

    D. Ethnic background

Answer: B. Experiential background
A person's culture has little to do with gender, social class, or ethnicity. A person is the product of his experiences. Acculturation is defined as: differences in experiential background.

62. To which aspect does fair assessment relate?
    (Easy)

    A. Representation

    B. Acculturation

    C. Language

    D. All of the above

Answer: D. All of the above
All three aspects are necessary and vital for assessment to be fair.

63. A test that measures students' skill development in academic content areas is classified as an _____ test.
    (Average)

    A. Achievement

    B. Aptitude

    C. Adaptive

    D. Intelligence

Answer: A. Achievement
Achievement tests directly assess students' skill development in academic content areas. They measure the degree to which a student has benefited from education and/or life experiences compared to others of the same age or grade level. They may be used as diagnostic tests to find strengths and weaknesses of students. They may also be used for screening, placement, progress evaluation, and curricular effectiveness.

64. Which of the following is an example of tactile perception?
    (Average)

    A. Making an angel in the snow with one's body

    B. Running a specified course

    C. Identifying a rough surface with eyes closed

    D. Demonstrating aerobic exercises

Answer: C. Identifying a rough surface with eyes closed
Tactile means having to do with touch.

65. **Which of the following activities best exemplifies a kinesthetic exercise in developing body awareness?**
    (Rigorous)

    A. Touching materials of different textures

    B. Playing a song and movement game like "Looby Loo"

    C. Identifying geometric shapes being drawn on one's back

    D. Making a shadow-box project

Answer: B. Playing a game like "Looby Loo"
Kinesthetic means having to do with body movement.

66. **Which of the following teaching activities is LEAST likely to enhance observational learning in students with special needs?**
    (Easy)

    A. A verbal description of the task to be performed, followed by having the children immediately attempt to perform the instructed behavior

    B. A demonstration of the behavior, followed by an immediate opportunity for the children to imitate the behavior

    C. A simultaneous demonstration and explanation of the behavior, followed by ample opportunity for the children to rehearse the instructed behavior

    D. Physically guiding the children through the behavior to be imitated, while verbally explaining the behavior

Answer: A. A verbal description of the task to be performed, followed by having the children immediately attempt to perform the instructed behavior
Students are given verbal instructions only. The children are not given a chance to observe or see the behavior so that they can imitate it. Some of the students may have hearing deficiencies. Others may need visual or kinesthetic cues to help them understand what is wanted of them.

67. The _____ modality is most frequently used in the learning process.
   (Average)

   A. Auditory

   B. Visual

   C. Tactile

   D. All of the Above

Answer: D. All of the above
The auditory, visual, and tactile modalities are the ones frequently used in the learning process. We learn through an integration of these modalities (multi-sensory approach).

68. Public Law 99-457 amended the EHA to make provisions for:
   (Easy)

   A. Education services for "uneducable" children

   B. Education services for children in jail settings

   C. Special education benefits for children birth to five years

   D. Education services for medically-fragile children

Answer: C. Special education benefits for children birth to five years
P.L. 99-457 amended EHA to provide special education programs for children 3-5 years, with most states offering outreach programs to identify children with special needs from birth to age 3.

69. Some environmental elements that influence the effectiveness of learning styles include all EXCEPT:
(Easy)

- A. Light
- B. Temperature
- C. Design
- D. Motivation

Answer: D. Motivation
Individual learning styles are influenced by environmental, emotional, sociological, and physical elements. Environmental elements include sound, light, temperature, and design. Emotional elements include motivation, persistence, responsibility, and structure. Motivation is not an environmental element.

70. In order for a student to function independently in the learning environment, which of the following must be true?
(Average)

- A. The learner must understand the nature of the content.
- B. The student must be able to do the assigned task.
- C. The teacher must communicate performance criteria to the learner.
- D. All of the above

Answer: D. All of the above
Together with the above, the child must be able to ask for and obtain assistance if necessary.

71. **What can a teacher plan that will allow him/her to avoid adverse situations with students?**
    (Rigorous)

    A. Instructional techniques

    B. Instructional materials and formats

    C. Physical setting and environment

    D. All of the above

Answer: D. All of the above
It is the teacher's responsibility to select instructional practices that reflect students' individual learning needs and to incorporate a wide range of learning strategies and specialized materials to meet those needs. Students display preferences for certain learning styles, and these differences are also factors in the teacher's choice of presentation and materials. Physical settings, instructional arrangements, materials available, and presentation techniques, are all factors under the teacher's control and can be manipulated to meet student needs.

72. **John learns best through the auditory channel, so his teacher wants to reinforce his listening skills. Through which of the following types of equipment would instruction be most effectively presented?**
    (Easy)

    A. Overhead projector

    B. Audio recording device

    C. Microcomputer

    D. Opaque projector

Answer: B. Audio recording device
An audio recording device, such as a voice recorder or an Ipod, would help sharpen and further develop his listening skills as he is an auditory learner.

73. **When teaching a student who is predominantly auditory to read, it is best to:**
    (Rigorous)

    A. Stress sight vocabulary

    B. Stress phonetic analysis

    C. Stress the shape and configuration of the word

    D. Stress rapid reading

Answer: B. Stress phonetic analysis
Sensory modalities are one of the physical elements that affect learning style. Some students learn best through their visual sense (sight), others through their auditory sense (hearing), and still others by doing, touching, and moving (tactile-kinesthetic). Auditory learners generally listen to people, follow verbal directions, and enjoy hearing records, cassette tapes, and stories. Phonics has to do with sound, an auditory stimulus. Since phonics involves attaching sounds to letters, visual stimuli, the child will need to integrate the two modalities. An auditory learner will start with the sounds, then move to visual cues.

74. **If a student is predominantly a visual learner, he may learn more effectively by:**
    (Easy)

    A. Reading aloud while studying

    B. Listening to a cassette tape

    C. Watching a video clip

    D. Using body movement

Answer: C. Watching a video clip
Visual learners use their sense of sight, which is the sense being used to watch a video clip.

75. A prerequisite skill is:
    (Average)

    A. The lowest order skill in a hierarchy of skills needed to perform a specific task

    B. A skill that must be demonstrated before instruction on a specific task can begin

    C. A tool for accomplishing task analysis

    D. The smallest component of any skill

Answer: B. A skill that must be demonstrated before instruction on a specific task can begin
This is an enabling skill that a student needs in order to perform an objective successfully.

76. Under the provisions of IDEA, the student is entitled to all of these EXCEPT:
    (Easy)

    A. Placement in the best environment

    B. Placement in the least restrictive environment

    C. Provision of educational needs at no cost

    D. Provision of individualized, appropriate educational program

Answer: A. Placement in the best environment
IDEA mandates a least restrictive environment, an IEP (individual education plan), and a free public education.

77. All of the following are suggestions for altering the presentation of tasks to match the student's rate of learning EXCEPT:
(Average)

    A.   Teach in several shorter segments of time rather than a single lengthy session.

    B.   Continue to teach a task until the lesson is completed in order to provide more time on task.

    C.   Watch for nonverbal cues that indicate students are becoming confused, bored, or restless.

    D.   Avoid giving students an inappropriate amount of written work.

Answer: B. Continue to teach a task until the lesson is completed in order to provide more time on task.
This action taken does not alter the subject content; neither does it alter the rate at which tasks are presented.

78. Which of the following is a good example of a generalization?
(Rigorous)

    A.   Jim has learned to add and is now ready to subtract.

    B.   Sarah adds sets of units to obtain a product.

    C.   Bill recognizes a vocabulary word on a billboard when traveling.

    D.   Jane can spell the word "net" backwards to get the word "ten."

Answer: C. Bill recognizes a vocabulary word on a billboard when traveling.
Generalization is the occurrence of a learned behavior in the presence of a stimulus other than the one that produced the initial response. It is the expansion of a student's performance beyond the initial setting. Students must be able to expand or transfer what is learned to other settings (e.g., reading to math word problems, resource room to regular classroom). Generalization may be enhanced by the following:
- Use many examples in teaching to deepen application of learned skills.
- Use consistency in initial teaching situations and later introduce variety in format, procedure, and use of examples.
- Have the same information presented by different teachers, in different settings, and under varying conditions.
- Include a continuous reinforcement schedule at first, later changing to delayed and intermittent schedules as instruction progresses.
- Teach students to record instances of generalization and to reward themselves at that time.
- Associate naturally occurring stimuli when possible.

79. Students who can recognize and name some letters and apply sounds to many of the consonants, and can do some invented spelling, but do not recognize common spelling patterns are in which phase of learning to decode?
(Average)

   A.   Pre-alphabetic phase

   B.   Partial alphabetic phase

   C.   Full- alphabetic phase

   D.   Consolidated alphabetic phase

Answer: B. Partial alphabetic phase
Ehri's five stages of alphabetic knowledge are:

1. **Pre-alphabetic phase**: Children respond to words as visual gestalts in context by memorizing their visual features, but don't yet understand phoneme/letter correspondence. They might recognize the word "stop" inside the usual hexagon shaped sign, but not recognize it in connected text.
2. **Partial-alphabetic phase:** Children can name some letters of the alphabet, apply sounds to many of the consonants. They can identify more words in different contexts, but cannot handle vowel sounds well and don't recognize common spelling patterns.
3. **Full-alphabetic phase:** Children have a good understanding of the graphophonemic system and fully grasp the connection between graphemes and phonemes. They can decode letter by letter and spell phonetically. They can decode unfamiliar words and store sight words in memory.
4. **Consolidated-alphabetic phase:** Children tend to see words as whole units and use all their decoding skills in unison to decode unfamiliar words, allowing them to decode multi-syllable words and decode words by analogy. At this stage they can also use such things as prefixes and suffixes as clues to decoding new words.
5. **Automatic phase:** At this phase, the child's decoding has reached a state of automaticity where word-level reading predominates, and reading is fluent and comprehension rivals that of listening comprehension.

80. **The following words all describe an IEP objective EXCEPT:**
    (Easy)

    A. Specific

    B. Observable

    C. Measurable

    D. Criterion-referenced

Answer: D. Criterion-referenced
An Individualized Education Plan (IEP) should be specific, observable, and measurable.

81. **Alan has failed repeatedly in his academic work. He needs continuous feedback in order to experience small, incremental achievements. What type of instructional material would best meet this need?**
    (Rigorous)

    A. Programmed materials

    B. Audiotapes

    C. Materials with no writing required

    D. Worksheets

Answer: A. Programmed materials
Programmed materials are best suited, as Alan would be able to chart his progress as he achieves each goal. He can monitor himself and take responsibility for his successes.

82. After purchasing what seemed to be a very attractive new math kit for use with her SLD (specific learning disabled) students, Ms. Davis discovered her students could not use the kit unless she read the math problems and instructions to them, as the readability level was higher than the majority of the students' functional reading capabilities. Which criterion of the materials selection did Ms. Davis most likely fail to consider when selecting this math kit?
    (Average)

    A. Durability

    B. Relevance

    C. Component parts

    D. Price

Answer: B. Relevance
Relevance is the only cognitive factor listed. Since her students were severely learning disabled, she almost certainly would have considered the kit's durability and component parts. She did not have to consider price, as that would be taken care of by the district. To be fully relevant to a population, the material must be *accessible* to the population, and the reading level of the material made it inaccessible to her students.

83. Which of the following questions most directly evaluates the utility of instructional material?
    (Rigorous)

    A. Is the cost within budgetary means?

    B. Can the materials withstand handling by students?

    C. Are the materials organized in a useful manner?

    D. Are the needs of the students met by the use of the materials?

Answer: C. Are the materials organized in a useful manner?
It is a question of utility or usefulness.

84. A money bingo game was designed by Ms. Johnson for use with her middle grade students. Cards were constructed with different combinations of coins pasted on each of the nine spaces. Ms. Johnson called out various amounts of change (e.g., 30 cents), and students were instructed to cover the coin combinations on their cards, which equaled the amount of change (e.g., two dimes and two nickels, three dimes, and so on). The student who had the first bingo was required to add the coins in each of the spaces covered and tell the amounts before being declared the winner. Five of Ms. Johnson's sixth graders played the game during the ten-minute free activity time following math the first day the game was constructed. Which of the following attributes are present in this game in this situation?
    (Average)

    A.   Accompanied by simple, uncomplicated rules

    B.   Of brief duration, permitting replay

    C.   Age appropriateness

    D.   All of the above

Answer: D. All of the above
Games and puzzles should also be colorful and appealing, of relevance to individual students, and appropriate for learners at different skill levels in order to sustain interest and motivational value.

85. According to the three tier RTI model described by the Florida Center for Reading Research's (FCRR), students who need a moderate amount of help in one of the five critical areas of reading instruction in a general education class would receive additional reading instruction through the:
(Average)

   A.   Core reading program

   B.   Intensive Intervention program

   C.   Modified Reading program

   D.   Supplemental reading program

Answer: D. Supplemental Reading Program.
Supplemental intervention programs provide help in one of the five critical areas of reading instruction: phonemic awareness, phonics, fluency, vocabulary, or comprehension. Children who have moderate needs will be in a second "tier" of assistance and will receive additional reading instruction each day. The intent is that these programs can be used to differentiate reading instruction in a general education setting, either through small group or individual work with the teacher or through additional staff assistance. The core reading program is the main program through which most children successfully achieve reading goals. Children who are two or more years behind grade level and who need much smaller group instruction or individual instruction on a much more intensive level, are in "tier 3," the *Intensive Intervention Program.*

86. Modifications of course material may take the form of:
(Average)

   A.   Simplifying texts

   B.   Parallel curriculum

   C.   Taped textbooks

   D.   All of the above

Answer: D. All of the above
Materials, usually textbooks, are frequently modified because of reading level. The goal of modification is to present the material in a manner that the student can more readily understand, while preserving the basic ideas and content.

87. **At which level of mathematics instruction will a child need to spend the most instructional and exploratory time in order to successfully master objectives?**
    (Average)

    A. Symbolic Level

    B. Concept Level

    C. Mastery Level

    D. Connecting Level

Answer: B. Concept Level.
In order to internalize the concept, the child needs repeated and varied interaction with manipulatives at the concept level. it is important that, wherever possible, the child be led to *discover* the concept rather than having it stated by the teacher, then trying to memorize it. Following this stage, the child can begin to apply labels and representations *along with the manipulatives.* This stage forms a bridge, or *connecting level* to the last stage, the *symbolic level* when the child has internalized the concepts behind the symbols and can manipulate them to learn more without the support of more concrete scaffolding.

88. **Which of the following statements is NOT offered as a rationale for inclusion?**
    (Rigorous)

    A. Special education students are not usually identified until their learning problems have become severe.

    B. Lack of funding will mean that support for the special needs children will not be available in the regular classroom.

    C. Putting children in segregated special education placements is stigmatizing.

    D. There are students with learning or behavior problems who do not meet special education requirements but who still need special services.

Answer: B. Lack of funding will mean that support for special needs children will not be available in the regular classroom.
All except lack of funding were offered in support of inclusion.

89. **Janice requires occupational therapy and speech therapy services. She is your student. What must you do to insure her services are met?**
(Rigorous)

   A. Watch the services being rendered.

   B. Schedule collaboratively.

   C. Ask for services to be given in a push-in model.

   D. Ask them to train you to give the service.

Answer: B. Schedule collaboratively.
Collaborative scheduling of students to receive services is both your responsibility and that of the service provider. Scheduling together allows for both your convenience and that of the service provider. It also will provide you with an opportunity to make sure the student does not miss important information.

90. **What can you do to create a good working environment with a classroom assistant?**
(Rigorous)

   A. Plan lessons with the assistant.

   B. Write a contract that clearly defines his/her responsibilities in the classroom.

   C. Remove previously given responsibilities.

   D. All of the above

Answer: A. Plan lessons with the assistant.
Planning with your classroom assistant shows that you respect his/her input and allows you to see where he/she feels confident.

91. **A paraprofessional has been assigned to assist you in the classroom. What action on the part of the teacher would lead to a poor working relationship?**
    (Average)

    A. Having the paraprofessional lead a small group

    B. Telling the paraprofessional what you expect him/her to do

    C. Defining classroom behavior management as your responsibility alone

    D. Taking an active role in his/her evaluation

Answer: C. Defining classroom behavior management as your responsibility alone
When you do not allow another adult in the room to enforce the class rules, you create an environment where the other adult is seen as someone not to be respected. No one wants to be in a work environment where they do not feel respected.

92. **Jonathan has Attention Deficit Hyperactivity Disorder (ADHD). He is in a regular classroom and appears to be doing okay. However, his teacher does not want John in her class because he will not obey her when she asks him to stop doing a repetitive action such as tapping his foot. The teacher sees this as distracting during tests. John needs:**
    (Easy)

    A. An IEP

    B. A 504 Plan

    C. A VESID evaluation

    D. A more restrictive environment

Answer: B. A 504 Plan
John is exhibiting normal grade level behavior with the exception of the ADHD behaviors, which may need some acceptance for his academic success. John has not shown any academic deficiencies. John needs a 504 Plan to provide small adaptations to meet his needs. These would be accommodations that would allow alternative behaviors that would meet his ADHD needs without distracting his classmates (e.g., wiggle seat, pillow or sponge to tap on, other "fiddle objects).

93. **In which way is a computer like an effective teacher?**
    (Average)

    A.   Provides immediate feedback

    B.   Sets the pace at the rate of the average student

    C.   Produces records of errors made only

    D.   Programs to skill levels at which students at respective chronological ages should be working

Answer: A. Provides immediate feedback
The computer is a good tool for providing immediate feedback to the student. Immediate feedback increases motivation and lessens the risk that the student will practice the wrong answers.

94. **A Behavioral Intervention Plan (BIP):**
    (Rigorous)

    A.   Should be written by a team.

    B.   Should be reviewed annually.

    C.   Should be written by the teacher who is primarily responsible for the student.

    D.   Should consider placement.

Answer: A. Should be written by a team.
IDEA 2004 establishes that the BIP is a team intervention. Writing BIPs without a team approach does not allow the behavior to truly be addressed as a team.

95. **Bill talks out in class an average of 15 times an hour. Other youngsters sometimes talk out, but Bill does so as a higher:**
    (Easy)

    A. Rate

    B. Intensity

    C. Volume

    D. Degree

Answer: A. Rate
Rate or frequency is the number of times the behavior is displayed in a given period.

96. **Which category of behaviors would most likely be found on a behavior rating scale?**
    (Easy)

    A. Disruptive, acting out

    B. Shy, withdrawn

    C. Aggressive (physical or verbal)

    D. All of the above

Answer: D. All of the above
These are all possible problem behaviors that can adversely impact the student or the class; thus, they may be found on behavior rating scales.

97. IDEA 2004 states that there are a disproportionate number of minority students classified as needing special education services. IDEA 2004 suggests that this is due to:
(Average)

   A. Socioeconomic status where disproportionate numbers exist

   B. Improper evaluations – Not making allowances for students who have English as a second language

   C. Growing population of minorities

   D. Percentage of drug abuse per ethnicity

Answer: B. Improper evaluations – Not making allowances for students who have English as a second language
IDEA 2004 questioned the acceptance or inclusion of students who have English as a second language as being over represented. The fact that a child's native language is not English is not a disability.

98. Bob shows behavior problems like lack of attention, being out of his seat, and talking out. His teacher has kept data on these behaviors and has found that Bob is showing much better self-control since he has been self-managing himself through a behavior modification program. The most appropriate placement recommendation for Bob at this time is probably:
(Easy)

   A. Any available part-time special education program

   B. The regular classroom solely

   C. A behavior disorders resource room for one period a day

   D. A specific learning disabilities resource room for one period a day

Answer: B. The regular classroom solely
Bob is able to self-manage himself and is very likely to behave like the other children in the regular classroom. The classroom is the least restrictive environment.

99. A Behavior Intervention Plan (BIP) is based on the behaviorist assumption that many problem behaviors are:
(Average)

    A.   Predictable

    B.   Observed

    C.   Conditioned

    D.   Learned

Answer: D. Learned
Behavior modification is based on the premise that most behavior, regardless of its appropriateness, has been learned, and therefore, can be changed.

100. Procedures employed to decrease targeted behaviors include:
(Rigorous)

    A.   Punishment

    B.   Negative reinforcement

    C.   Shaping

    D.   Both A and B

Answer: A. Punishment
Punishment and extinction may be used to decrease target behaviors.

101. Target behaviors must be:
(Easy)

    A.   Observable

    B.   Measurable

    C.   Definable

    D.   All of the above

Answer: D. All of the above
Behaviors must be observable, measurable, and definable in order to be assessed and changed.

102. The most important step in writing a Functional Behavioral Assessment (FBA) is:
(Rigorous)

    A.   Establish a replacement behavior.

    B.   Establish levels of interventions.

    C.   Establish antecedents related or causative to the behavior.

    D.   Establish assessment periods of FBA effectiveness.

Answer: C. Establish antecedents related or causative to the behavior.
An FBA will only be successful if antecedents are recognized. Avoidance of situations and training/cultivating of replacement behaviors then become possible.

103. Which description best characterizes primary reinforcers of an edible nature?
(Average)

    A.   Natural

    B.   Unconditioned

    C.   Innately motivating

    D.   All of the above

Answer: D. All of the above
Primary reinforcers are those stimuli that are of biological importance to an individual. They are natural, unlearned, unconditioned, and innately motivating. The most common and appropriate reinforcer used in the classroom is food.

104. Mrs. Chang is trying to prevent satiation from occurring so that her reinforcers will be effective, as she is using a continuous reinforcement schedule. Which of the following ideas would be LEAST effective in preventing satiation?
(Rigorous)

    A.   Use only one type of edible rather than a variety.

    B.   Ask for ten vocabulary words rather than twenty.

    C.   Give pieces of cereal, bits of fruit, or M&Ms rather than large portions of edibles.

    D.   Administer a peanut then a sip of water.

Answer: A. Use only one type of edible rather than a variety.
Here are some suggestions for preventing satiation:
- Vary reinforcers with instructional tasks.
- Shorten the instructional sessions, and presentation of reinforcers will be decreased.
- Alternate reinforcers (e.g., food, then juice).
- Decrease the size of edibles presented.
- Have an array of edibles available.

105. Which tangible reinforcer would Mr. Whiting find to be MOST effective with teenagers?
(Easy)

    A.   Plastic whistle

    B.   Winnie-the-Pooh book

    C.   Poster of a current rock star

    D.   Toy ring

Answer: C. Poster of a current rock star
This tops the list of things that teenagers crave. It is the most desirable.

106. A positive reinforcer is generally effective if it is desired by the student and is:
(Easy)

    A.   Worthwhile in size

    B.   Given immediately after the desired behavior

    C.   Given only upon the occurrence of the target behavior

    D.   All of the above

Answer: D. All of the above
Timing and quality of the reinforcer are key to encouraging the individual to continue the targeted behavior.

107. Dispensing school supplies is a component associated with which type of reinforcement system?
(Average)

    A.   Activity reinforcement

    B.   Tangible reinforcement

    C.   Token reinforcement

    D.   Both B and C

Answer: A. Activity reinforcement
The Premack Principle states that any activity in which a student voluntarily participates on a frequent basis can be used as a reinforcer for any activity in which the student seldom participates. Running errands, decorating bulletin boards, leading group activities, passing out books or papers, collecting materials, or operating equipment all provide activity reinforcement.

108. Which type of reinforcement system is most easily generalized into other settings?
(Average)

- A. Social reinforcement
- B. Activity reinforcement
- C. Tangible reinforcement
- D. Token reinforcement

Answer: A. Social reinforcement
There are many advantages to social reinforcement. It is easy to use, takes little of the teacher's time or effort, and is available in any setting. It is always positive, unlikely to satiate, and can be generalized to most situations.

109. NCLB and IDEA 2004 changed special education teacher requirements by:
(Easy)

- A. Requiring a highly-qualified status for job placement
- B. Adding changes to the requirement for certifications
- C. Adding legislation requiring teachers to maintain knowledge of law
- D. Requiring inclusive environmental experience prior to certification

Answer: A. Requiring a highly-qualified status for job placement
NCLB and IDEA 2004 place a requirement that all teachers shall be equally qualified to teach in their content areas.

110. In the Grammatic Closure subtest of the Illinois Test of Psycholinguistic Abilities, the child is presented with a picture representing statements such as the following: "Here is one die; here are two ____." This test is essentially a test of:
(Rigorous)

    A.   Phonology

    B.   Syntax

    C.   Morphology

    D.   Semantics

Answer: C. Morphology
Morphology refers to the rules governing the structure of words and how to put morphemes together to make words. "Dice" is the irregular plural form of "Die." Changing the ending to 'ce' is using a morphological structure. Syntax is a system of rules for sentence formation, not word formation.

111. Which law specifically states that, "Full Inclusion is not the only way for a student to reach his/her highest potential"?
(Rigorous)

    A.   IDEA

    B.   IDEA 97

    C.   IDEA 2004

    D.   Part 200

Answer: C. IDEA 2004
In IDEIAA (IDEA 2004), stated that full inclusion was not always best for the individual student. A small number of students may need much smaller group instruction, highly specialized or extensive instruction techniques, or a more protected environment. For such students, a smaller, substantially separate class may be "least restrictive" *for them.* This allows students who need a different setting in order to learn to be served appropriately in a more "restrictive" setting when people who push full inclusion are confronted. Of course, it is necessary in such situations to attend to the child's social needs and ensure that the child is included with peers to the greatest extent possible given the specific disabilities and needs involved.

112. Which of the following is untrue about the ending "er"?
(Rigorous)

    A.   It is an example of a free morpheme.

    B.   It represents one of the smallest units of meaning within a word.

    C.   It is called an inflectional ending.

    D.   When added to a word, it connotes a comparative status.

Answer: A. It is an example of a free morpheme.
A morpheme is the smallest unit of meaningful language. A free morpheme has meaning that can stand alone as a word. "Er," on its own, has no meaning. It is a bound morpheme, and is affixed to a free morpheme to alter its meaning.

113. NCLB (No Child Left Behind Act) was signed on January 8, 2002. It addresses what?
(Rigorous)

    A.   Accessibility of curriculum to the student

    B.   Administrative incentives for school improvements

    C.   The funding to provide services required

    D.   Accountability of school personnel for student achievement

Answer: D. Accountability of school personnel for student achievement
School personnel are responsible for teaching grade appropriate curriculum goals with modifications and accommodations for students' disabilities and special needs. This may require using entry level objectives or alternative assessment methods, as well.

114. **The social skills of students in intellectual disabilities programs are likely to be appropriate for children of their mental age, rather than chronological age. This means that the teacher will need to do all of the following EXCEPT:**
(Easy)

    A.   Model desired behavior.

    B.   Provide clear instructions.

    C.   Expect age-appropriate behaviors.

    D.   Adjust the physical environment when necessary.

Answer: C. Expect age-appropriate behaviors
Age appropriate means mental age appropriate, not chronological age appropriate.

115. **Which of the following is a language disorder?**
(Average)

    A.   Articulation problems

    B.   Stuttering

    C.   Aphasia

    D.   Excessive Nasality

Answer: C. Aphasia
Language disorders are often considered just one category of speech disorder. The problem is really different, with its own origins and causes. Persons with language disorders exhibit one or more of the following traits:
- Difficulty in comprehending questions, commands, or statements (receptive language problems)
- Inability to adequately express their own thoughts (expressive language problems)
- Language that is below the level expected for the child's chronological age (delayed language)
- Interrupted language development (dysphasia)
- Qualitatively different language
- Total absence of language

116. Which of the following is a speech disorder?
(Average)

   A.   Dysfluency

   B.   Aphasia

   C.   Delayed language

   D.   Comprehension difficulties

Answer: A. Dysfluency
Persons with speech disorders exhibit one or more of the following traits:
- Unintelligible speech or speech that is difficult to understand, and articulation disorders (distortions, omissions, substitutions)
- Speech-flow disorders (sequence, duration, rate, rhythm, fluency)
- Unusual voice quality (nasality, breathiness, hoarseness, pitch, intensity, quality disorders)
- Obvious emotional discomfort when trying to communicate (stuttering, cluttering)
- Damage to nerves or brain centers which control muscles used in speech (dysarthria).

117. Which of the following is an example of cross-modal perception involving integrating visual stimuli to an auditory verbal process?
(Rigorous)

   A.   Following spoken directions

   B.   Describing a picture

   C.   Finding certain objects in pictures

   D.   Both B and C

Answer: B. Describing a picture
We see (visual modality) the picture and use words (auditory modality) to describe it.

118. Matthew's conversational speech is adequate, but when he tries to speak before a group of more than two listeners, his speech becomes mumbling and halting. Which of the following activities would be LEAST helpful in strengthening Matthew's self-expression skills?
(Rigorous)

   A.   Having him participate in show-and-tell time

   B.   Asking him comprehension questions about a story that was read to the class

   C.   Having him recite a poem in front of the class, with two other children

   D.   Asking him to tell a joke to the rest of the class

Answer: B. Asking him comprehension questions about a story that was read to class.
Answering the teacher's questions emphasizes speaking in front of one other person (the teacher) and does not expand his comfort zone to a larger group. The other activities require him to speak in front of more people.

119. All of the modes listed below are primary categories of Augmentative Alternative Communication EXCEPT:
(Easy)

   A.   Wheelchairs

   B.   Graphical communication boards

   C.   Eye gaze techniques

   D.   Sign language

Answer: A. Wheelchairs
The primary purpose of a wheelchair is mobility, not communication.

120. A functional curriculum includes:
(Average)

- A. Regents curriculum
- B. Life skills
- C. Remedial academics
- D. Vocational placement

Answer: B. Life skills
While a, c and, d may be utilized in the functional curriculum, the curriculum may not be considered functional without addressing life skills.

POST-TEST ANSWER KEY

1. C
2. A
3. D
4. A
5. C
6. C
7. D
8. A
9. D
10. B
11. C
12. B
13. C
14. C
15. B
16. A
17. D
18. D
19. A
20. D
21. C
22. A
23. B
24. A
25. D
26. B
27. C
28. A
29. B
30. B
31. C
32. B
33. A
34. D
35. C
36. D
37. D
38. B
39. A
40. C
41. D
42. A
43. C
44. C

45. C
46. D
47. C
48. C
49. A
50. C
51. C
52. D
53. C
54. B
55. B
56. D
57. A
58. D
59. C
60. B
61. B
62. D
63. A
64. C
65. B
66. A
67. D
68. C
69. D
70. D
71. D
72. B
73. B
74. C
75. B
76. A
77. B
78. C
79. B
80. D
81. A
82. B
83. C
84. D
85. D
86. D
87. B
88. B

89. B
90. A
91. C
92. B
93. A
94. A
95. A
96. D
97. B
98. B
99. D
100. A
101. D
102. C
103. D
104. A
105. C
106. D
107. A
108. A
109. A
110. C
111. C
112. A
113. D
114. C
115. C
116. A
117. B
118. B
119. A
120. B

POST-TEST RIGOR TABLE

	Easy 28%	Average 36%	Rigorous 36%
Question	12, 14, 17, 18, 21, 22, 25, 26, 28, 36, 38, 42, 48, 54, 55, 58, 62, 66, 68, 69, 72, 74, 76, 80, 92, 95, 96, 98, 101, 105, 106, 109, 114, 119	2, 6, 7, 13, 16, 19, 20, 24, 27, 31, 32, 37, 40, 41, 44, 49, 51, 52, 53, 56, 60, 63, 64, 67, 70, 75, 77, 79, 82, 84, 85, 86, 87, 91, 93, 97, 99, 103, 107, 108, 115, 116, 120	1, 3, 4, 5, 8, 9, 10, 11, 15, 23, 29, 30, 33, 34, 35, 39, 43, 45, 46, 47, 50, 57, 59, 61, 65, 71, 73, 78, 81, 83, 88, 89, 90, 94, 100, 102, 104, 110, 111, 112, 113, 117, 118

More Study Tools to Help Pass Your Certification Exam

XAMonline.com

Pass your exam with our suite of superior study tools, including:

- Print books
- eBooks
- eFlashcards
- Web-based interactive study guides

Teaching in another state? XAMonline carries 500+ state-specific and PRAXIS study guides covering every test subject nationwide.

Call or visit us online!
800.301.4647 | www.XAMonline.com

CPSIA information can be obtained
at www.ICGtesting.com
Printed in the USA
BVHW04s0746080318
509962BV00022B/46/P